YOUR LIFE

A Practical guide to Happiness, Peace and Fulfillment

Hina Hashmi

For Betterment Publications
INCREASING SUCCESS AND HAPPINESS
United States • United Kingdom
Canada • Europe • India

Your Life: A Practical guide to Happiness, Peace and Fulfilment.

Text and illustrations copyright © 2014 Hina Hashmi

First published in the United Kingdom in 2014 by For Betterment Publications

The right of Hina Hashmi (Hina Hashmi) to be identified as the Author of the Work has been asserted by him in accordance with the Copyright, Designs and Patents Act 1988.

Disclaimer

Every effort has been made to make this book as accurate as possible. However, the text should be used only as a general guide and not as the ultimate source of the subject matter covered. The author shall have neither liability nor responsibility to any person or entity with respect to any loss or damage caused or alleged to be caused directly or indirectly by the information covered in this book.

DEDICATION

To all those who are open to learning and changing
their lives for good.

Table of Contents

ACKNOWLEDGEMENTS

I pay gratitude to 'One Universal' power which always supports and loves me unconditionally. He is/has been the only support in my lonely, depressing, disappointing and painful moments of life. The one whom I trust blindly which I can't do for human beings. Thank You for showing me the way of truth and faith, and helping me in finding my true purpose. Thanks for being with me every day when I struggle between 'Faith' and 'Fear'. I am highly thankful for the wisdom which you sent to me via intuition and made me able to write this book which has a potential to make a difference in reader's life. Thank You for connecting me with great people.

I am very much thankful to my parents who loved and supported me throughout my life. I may not have been able to complete this book without their help, prayers and love.

To my Little sister Bushra for her love and care for me.
To my dear friends who believe in me genuinely, care and motivate me.
To all those authors who wrote the books I read and learned how to make life better. The trainers, coaches and speakers who impacted my life via seminars, training programmes and home-study courses.
To my clients who supported me with their love, care and encouragement.
To my body for its support, bearing my negative emotions and carelessness.
Special thanks to the people who were bad to me with the intention to make me suffer. They motivated me to find ways to change my life in a positive way.

A Note for You

Well done for committing to personal growth, knowledge and the quest to understand the working of life. Very few people chose to learn something beyond their college curriculum. Being an academic person I spent 20 years of my life completing degrees and certifications because I believed that qualifications gave prestige, money, honor significance and happiness. And I got everything except happiness, peace and health. Nobody taught me how to find happiness in little things in life and to be contented. I thought life was all about achieving targets as I was in continuous race of achieving more and competing with others.

My story isn't like the usual motivational gurus have but it's the other way round. I was brought up in a very luxurious environment. Servants, chauffer driven cars, large private on-suite, big gardens and what not. Just imagine how it would have felt to live in a tiny room in a shared house after landing in the U.K. and the cultural shock was big too. I was raised in a religious family, offered prayers regularly and often participated in religious ceremonies but I felt none of my prayers were answered how I wanted them to be. I always believed in the one universal power. Being a child I thought God doesn't like me because I never scored the grades, at school, which I wanted and my family expected of me. I always tried different ways of praying (and begging) but the results were same! Then I developed a belief that I shouldn't expect anything good in life!

Needless to say, this belief made me depressed, frustrated and angry.

My relationships were full of pain because of my passive personality and the fear of losing nice people. Another reason was me being too emotional dependent on friends. A lot of them used me (for money and other materialistic purposes) and treated me as a doormat.

I studied and taught psychology for more than 10 years but didn't find answers for my problems in life. Believe me, most of the psychologists, psychiatrists and mental health professionals don't really implement what they learn.

I always thought why I don't get instant return of my good deeds from the people whom I cared/sacrificed for? I used to ask God, why do negative people win in every situation whether it's college, work place or family affairs? I felt frustrated and angry for this injustice.

I was surrounded by energy vampires who were sucking my happiness and freedom. I always blamed myself for allowing people to enter my life and hurt me.

Although I lived a luxurious life, I couldn't feel the love and connection with my closed ones because my mind was always looking for flaws. I never trained it to focus on the positive qualities of people or to thank for all that I had.

As the days and months passed, my questions increased and created more confusion in my life. I was always open to any information which could help me thus I studied almost every type of psychotherapy. I completed five degrees in psychology. Yes, you read it right, but some of my questions still weren't answered! Five years ago I started studying personal development books. I have read almost 150 books including motivational, religious, spiritual, inspirational, the universal laws for life and everything that I could find on the subject including blogs, magazines, the writings of the old philosophers and the new psychologists, audios & video programs...

and attended many seminars, and attended courses in different alternative therapies.

My life didn't turn around in one day. Whenever I learned new things, which were implemented by the successful and happy people, I tried to apply them in my life. Many times I felt disappointed, hopeless, disturbed and experienced physical health problems. My self esteem was low too. I used to fight with myself for why I was not experiencing happiness. I was frustrated because I wasn't getting instant results. Like many I always wanted instant gratification, was impatient and never felt gratitude in my heart. I wasn't aware of the fact that when you 'feel' thankful, not just say it, your complaints in life automatically reduce.

Often I got guidance from the universe for resolving the issues in my life i.e. I attracted books and courses which were perfect for specific phases of my life. The books I read had the answers for my problems and confusions at that time. I had a good habit of writing everything down.

I came to know that I had my own personal vibrations which were affecting all the areas of my life and this universe is actually 'energy' and we all are vibrating on a specific frequency. We are all responsible for everything in our lives i.e. we make choices and get results. There are times when we are given challenges in order to improve or to learn lessons from those painful events/situations.

After learning the law of attraction, like many, I was trying to manifest everything on my terms i.e. at my desired time and conditions. I made vision boards, created goals, repeated affirmations and had a positive vision *but* things weren't working my way! Why wasn't it working, even though I was following all the rules specified by personal development gurus? Why was I stuck? Once again I started blaming myself and my luck. A fulfilled life seemed far away. It doesn't mean things weren't working, but they were not on my terms. Life was showing me a mirror, I was manifesting in accordance with what I believed deep within and how I felt most of the time. One of my biggest mistakes was not being ready to learn from mistakes hence similar challenges kept showing up again and again for example I did affirmations and offered prayers to get rid of negative people but they kept connecting and at one point I was about to give up. But a wise person told me that the negative events will keep coming until I learn the lesson(s) and change my mind set. I realized that everyone has a purpose on earth. We are all connected and we need some cooperation of others in order to fulfill our dreams.

A lot of us are confused when it comes to fate and controlling our lives. Even after all those degrees and self-help books, I couldn't figure out the difference. Should we leave everything to fate/God/Universe/Divinity? Or should we take control of everything and design our lives in our own ways? I was using my will power to bring changes in my life.

Two years ago I decided to write what I learned from the world-renowned teachers, gurus, and successful people. I wish I knew when I was a teenager. My life could have been totally different. So I started writing what I understood about life and how small deeds can give us peace and happiness. It was a very interesting experience while writing because a lot of ideas were downloaded via intuition/inner-guidance. An important learning was that when I started to remove mental blocks, my intuition flowed fast.

Dreaming of a luxurious and rich life is very good. You must put all your efforts but it will happen at a certain time in your life because it depends upon your readiness, the beliefs you hold and the choices you make to become rich. This universe has enough for everyone, we don't need to snatch or harm other people's happiness in order to fulfill our desires.

I learned that forgiveness isn't an instant thing; it must be done on a regular basis otherwise anger would keep piling up which affects our personal vibration negatively.

I worked on my thoughts and beliefs extensively. I came to know that we must work on our soul too alongside our minds. By resolving mental blocks I developed sharp memory, started experiencing good mood often, peace of mind, physical healing, inner joy, and started accessing intuition.

Now, I get inner guidance through different ways like dreams, clairvoyance, premonition, lucid dreaming, and clairsentience. I know each and everything that is happening in the universe guides us and gives us message for us whether it's through animals, birds or events. I follow my intuition (gut feelings) for making day to day decisions like visiting a place or working with the new clients or choosing a vendor etc.

I do intuitive coaching sessions in which I read someone's life sometimes through their pictures and sometimes I can just read their auras while sitting far away. I think this is the greatest gift for someone who had lots of bad relationships and who couldn't understand people and their intentions.

Four years ago I couldn't even think about migrating to a country on my own because I had so many fears and limiting self-beliefs, and was raised in a conservative family but 3 years ago I came to the UK for higher studies and have been managing life in a country where the culture, language and lifestyle are very different. Honestly life isn't unfolding according to my plans even now. I planned a completely different life 4 years ago but I am happy, peaceful and living my passion. I believe that each and every day of my life will unfold before me and I just need to flow with it just by being appreciative, living in the present moment, having faith in the Universe/God and taking actions.

The purpose of our lives isn't just to get degrees, earn money, get married, having kids and live like a robot who just lives a typical life. After implementing what I learned from the best self-help and spiritual gurus I realized that inner-happiness, peace and freedom were not dependant on the luxurious life I had lived.

This book will help you to understand that taking the path of least resistance is always helpful and peaceful, which is always in line with your life's purpose for example if your purpose is to help people to be healthy like being a doctor or fitness consultant but you are doing something in the field of finance or engineering. If your current work area is different than your purpose then you will face extra challenges. May be you are successful in what you do but universe will keep trying to bring you back to your purpose. Divinity guides us all the time but most of us don't know how to interpret its messages.

The book explains how our energy shifts along with our thoughts about who we are, who others are in relation to us and even how we view the world in general (as harsh, uncaring, scarce, unforgiving, etc.) and how each experience effects our self-beliefs.

Other key concepts include our natural vibration, frequency and how we are all connected. How our perceptions creates our reality and how the laws of the universe effect our lives every single minute.

All these key facts about life have been mentioned in the ancient texts and most have been proven by quantum physics.

I feel sad when I see that most of us aren't aware of the laws of the universe, principles of happiness and success hence we believe that life is all about collecting material wealth, power and fame.

This is an easy to understand book with practical tips and techniques to make your life better. Explore yourself to answer the questions at the end of each chapter before moving on.

My passion is to share the facts, knowledge and techniques which I discovered in the past few years and decrease suffering in people's lives unlike the pain I went through due to unawareness of these principles.

You can choose to implement what you learn in this book or continue to believe in your old painful beliefs. You may have to read it more than once at various occasions if you wish to keep on living a better life.

May happiness, peace and fulfillment increase in your life.

Hina Hashmi

Hina Hashmi

16

SECTION NO: 1

If you want to find the secrets of the universe, think in terms of energy, frequency and vibration.

~Nikola Tesla

Understanding Vibrations & Energy

How do these Affect Your Daily Life and Manifestations of Your Desires?

"As is understood, Life - God - in its essence is Vibration."
~Edgar Cayce

Every human being is an extension of divine, and he is co-creating his universe, acquiring non physical part of himself with him. We are all a collection of vibrations and energy. Vibration is defined as the **thought pattern** in which we choose. Our vibrations are interpretation of our five senses i.e. sound, visual, smell, touch and taste. People of this planet are expanding it by their thoughts, because our world is shaping itself according to the thoughts of people. We are causing expansion of time-space reality. We are contributing hugely to this process.

Every time we ask, the universe provides. When you desire something you add it in your vibration. Even when you think of something negative you give energy to it. Any time that you've focused on what you didn't want, you are moving away from what you want. Saying 'no' can mean 'come to me' for example; war against terrorism will bring more war and terrorism rather than peace. Your positive vibrations will be a gift to future generations and vice versa.

We are two headed monsters. Anything that manifests was once a vibration.

Thought

↓

Thought Form

↓

Manifestation

Understanding Vibrations

Life like a Wave and Personal Vibrations

"To know the mechanics of the wave is to know the entire secret of nature."
~Walter Russell

Most people around us are perfectionists. They want everything in life at one time and try to stay happy at all time. Life has a wave like nature. We are vibrating beings and have individual vibrations that are called **personal vibration**. We are so lucky because we can influence it. Our vibration depends upon what we are thinking, feeling and acting. You have two choices, one is to go with chaotic frequencies of the world and feel hopeless, or decide what and how you want to feel.

If you chose the soul realm/super conscious realm (this will be explained later in section II) your personal vibrations maintain one point which is called "Your True frequency" (state of happiness, joy & peace) this also will be explained in section II. States of body, emotions, and thoughts are fluctuations in the vibration. At some point one shall experience and feel pain while in another, instance pleasure can be experienced. Don't react while you are upset because at that time your reaction will be based upon your current emotions; but when you are calm your thoughts will be intuitive and positive.

You can improve your overall vibration just by improving one part. If you are hopeless then feel contentment for a while. When you are sad change your state by going out for a walk or meditating.

Some people around us are energy vampires while others are energy boosters. Our bodies resonate like a tuning fork, that's why the vibration of others can affect our own vibration. If you meet someone who is sad sluggish, your body will immediately follow that pattern. Meeting an excited person can stimulate creativity inside you. You always have the power to choose your personal vibration.

"Right now and right now and right now and right now everybody has a mood or a feeling. Even if you don't even know that you have it, right now you all have a mood or feeling, and that mood or feeling is causing you to send off, or put out a vibration. And how many kinds are there? Two. And they're negative vibrations and positive vibrations. So that means right now, whether you all like it or not, or understand it or not, you are all emitting or putting off this vibration. There's only two kinds: negative or positive."
~Michael Losier

We all have a natural vibration which is a vibration of our soul. Every child has a bright and high frequency when he enters into this world. The soul is coated by the clutters of emotional and mental type. People feel good when they consider and prove themselves to be victims because they gain attention through it. They do it unconsciously and work at a low level of vibration due to the above given reasons. These low vibration people, places, and events will continue appearing in your life until you don't change these ideas.

Actually these limiting beliefs and thoughts are created in the mind. These mental blocks must be cleared to spend a happy time on earth. Loving wisdom of the soul opens for everyone after clearing of these mental blocks.

Effects of Electromagnetic Waves and Vibrations on Our Lives

We encounter **electromagnetic fields** every single day. Many invisible waves and vibrations cross in the space around us. Even the physical pains and emotional moods of other people around us affect our lives. Our souls match/mirror the vibrations of other people faster than our bodies.

You can feel the difference of vibration even at your home. You may feel better in your garden as compared to your TV lounge. The reason can be smoother energy in your garden. People who spend more time with machines have sleep problems because the energy emitted by machines disturbs our vibrations.

Sensitive people can identify soothing and disturbing energy, and health and unhealthy fields of vibration. They can even feel the frequency of the future events. Your body is your best guide i.e. it constantly tells you what's working for you and what's not.

We aren't solid beings living on this planet instead this planet is a collection of energies where all energies are penetrating each other.

Waves of Energy and States of Consciousness

All the vibrations, from lower to higher level, are waves of energy. States of the consciousness are the outcome of various brain wave activities. There are four types of brain waves and we experience all of them during sleep:

Beta (13-40 Hz) - are faster and present when we are awake and engaged in some kind of mental activity

Alpha (8-13 Hz) - are slower but not linked with drowsiness. These are generated when we meditate, day dream, visualize, relax, spend time in nature and while accessing intuition

Theta (4-8Hz) - are slower and linked with drowsiness. We can feel it while in a trance like state or have lost the track of time

Delta (1/2 4 Hz) - are very slow and are experienced during deep sleep.

These four stages are essential in understanding your true self.

Everything Around is Energy and Connected

"We are all connected; To each other, biologically. To the earth, chemically. To the rest of the universe atomically."
~Neil deGrasse Tyson

We aren't separate from the world and everything in the universe is connected. Our reality has been shaped by our perception. Solid things have energy particles inside them, called molecules and atomic particles, which continuously vibrate, are actually waves of energy. These particles can act as wave and particle simultaneously.

We are surrounded by a layer of energy called "**Aura**". Aura can be photographed and its density and colour can be measured. When we think and imagine our aura's colour changes depending on the quality of our thoughts. Everything around us is energy and nothing can be separated in terms of energy whether physical or non physical. Like the 'Law of conservation of energy' states that the total amount of energy in an isolated system remains constant over time, quantum physics derived that energy is neither created nor destroyed.

It's not possible to see everything physically. If you need money you need to tap into the higher vibration. Once it starts flowing, it can amaze you.

"If you want to find the secrets of the universe, think in terms of energy, frequency and vibration."
~Nikola Tesla

This world is an ocean of waves and vibrations. We are well aware that energy moves in waves. These waves are of different intensities and speeds which provide them with unique characteristics and behaviors. This energy wave needs a field, for example air, water etc to travel.

Electromagnetic waves can be divided in to low and high frequency waves. Low frequency waves have high wavelength while high frequency waves have a lower wavelength. The vibrations coming from earth influence our bodies. The seasons on earth, cycles of days and nights also show wave cycles. All species have to coordinate with them. Greg Braden reported that earth's base resonant frequency has increased from 7.8 cycles per second to 8.6 and climbing. It causes increase in pulse rate of earth which declines the magnetic field strength. During the last 4000 years it has lost half of its intensity. This can lead to a magnetic pole shift. Earth frequencies are linked to our cellular vibrations which bring evolutionary changes in DNA.

The benefit of this high intensity and less magnetic fields are the easy access to higher states of consciousness easily because old emotional and mental patterns will not be stored for a longer time. Waves of energy are travelling everywhere but we all are also vibrating. Our body is always oscillating. The most prominent oscillation is breathing, in which we take oxygen in while move carbon dioxide out. In the same way working of heart and electrical buzz of your brain are also vibrations in which charges of nerves are higher vibes. Deeper are the vibes of neurotransmitters and on the deepest level are the vibrations of molecules and atoms.

"We humans have always sought to increase our personal energy in the only manner we have known, by seeking to psychologically steal it from the others--an unconscious competition that underlies all human conflict in the world."
~James Redfield

We are not creating anything alone. All your dreams are coming true with the cooperation and co-creation of other souls. All other souls have to shift their desires to realize your dream. If you want to go to holiday, all other souls have to shift their needs for the fulfillment of your desire. It includes all people involved in your travelling, stay & everything you do during holidays. In some way it's beneficial for them as well. You can materialize what you want but not by depriving other souls. When you are confused about decision making that means this situation isn't helpful for your fellow souls. When you aren't open to grow; you are in fact creating hindrances in everyone's growth.

Store House

"Everything you are seeking is seeking you."
~Rumi

Every type of vibrations available in this universe e.g. positive & negative, vibration of fear, poverty, disease, failure, misery; and vibration of prosperity, health, success and happiness. Human beings attract vibrations which are in harmony with the dominating vibrations of their mind. Human beings always have a choice of going after positive or negative, prosperity or poverty, health or disease, success or fear.

Every Possibility Already Exists

"The visible world is the invisible organization of energy."
~Heinz Pagels

The universal mind has all knowledge, discoveries of the present and future. It's up to human beings when they access available resources, as these are waiting for them to move forward. We can attract almost anything by using our imagination. All we need to do is to hold the picture of desires/dreams in our mind and focus on it as it blends it with emotions that are of higher vibrations. Our frequencies will improve automatically. When you ask, feel and believe- you receive. You hold everything in your consciousness. There is an unlimited supply of ideas waiting for you to tap into and to bring forth.

Everything is an Expression of the Same Thing

"Everything you see has its roots in the unseen world. The forms may change, yet the essence remains the same. Every wonderful sight will vanish; every sweet word will fade, but do not be disheartened, the source they come from is eternal, growing, branching out, giving new life and new joy. Why do you weep? The source is within you and this whole world is springing up from it."
~Rumi

Law of vibrations states, that **"Everything is connected through vibrations"**. We cannot draw a line between rainbow colours. The amplitude of the specific vibration increases when we concentrate on that type of thoughts because selection of specific thoughts effect brain cells and they vibrate and send electronic waves. These waves become stronger by concentration. Learn to focus on the good aspects of a bad situation.

"The power of Thought, the magic of the Mind."
~Lord Byron

If your thoughts, feelings and actions are not in harmony of what you desire, you can't materialize it. Let's consider an example of driving a car —if you know all the theory but you haven't practiced then what are the chances of you driving properly? You have to practice it over and over again until the idea is fixed in your mind, until you develop sufficient brain cells to do it. Thinking is a skill which develops with the passage of time. We, usually, think in pictures, but actually our body is in control of our mind, 1000's of cells of mind pictures and images are imprinted every single day.

You have to develop brain cells for everything whether you want relationship, money or career success. John a student of class 7 in

Birmingham couldn't perform well, when his case was studied in detail, it was found that everybody including the teachers and parents labelled him as a "Bad Student". When the label of "Bad student" was removed with in very short period of time he performed extremely well and qualified for the scholarships.

When your mind is trained for something, it's easy for you to identify it e.g. If you haven't seen a spaceship you cannot identify what it is. Once you have seen it, you will be able to identify it easily. When you see something for the first time, new brain cells are developed for storing the new image(s).

Thinking about a certain idea moves brain cells in a specific direction and repetition increases the speed. Addition of beliefs and emotions impregnates cells with the characteristics of our idea. We have to just increase the frequency of positive thoughts that will increase our vibration and will move us in the direction of our desire.

The only difference in steam and ice is the state of vibration.

ICE   ⟶   STEAM
Where you are *(VIBRATION)*   where you want to go.

The only distance you have to travel towards your desires, is just a change in your vibrations. Depression is energy in a lower state of vibrations and success is energy in a higher state, happiness, joy is orderly vibration.

Happiness & Health   ⟶   *Higher Vibration*

If you are asked to make a picture in your mind about something pleasant, your state of vibrations will automatically change. Your enjoyment will increase while holding that concept for long. If you want to meet successful and positive people, you need to maintain these higher vibrations. Your inner world has complete power to transform your life by changing your outer world. Whatever you are searching for exists within you; you must learn to gain awareness about that.

"When you talk about what you want and why you want it, there's usually less resistance within you than when you talk about what you want and how you're going to get it. When you pose questions you don't have answers for, like how, where, when, who, it sets up a contradictory vibration that slows everything down."
~Abraham

If energy is neither created nor destroyed; everything you will ever want is already here. It is simply a matter of choosing the thoughts that will put you into harmonious vibration with what you desire.

A higher rate of vibration always destroys the lower rate of vibration. If we have negative things that we don't want, we need a goal in higher order of vibration. The thing you hate is yours; the thing you love is yours. If it's not in your physical world, it's present in your mental world.

HARMONY

↑

Go to higher order of vibration

Higher order vibration

Kills

↓

Lower order vibration

Know Thyself

Everyone is unique with different potentials and this universe is full of opportunities. The thought which may be right for you, may not be right for someone else. Variety is the one of basic human needs; we desire different things in different areas of life. Sometimes we aren't aware that we are asking and unconsciously send messages to the universe which may in return manifest. Now the source within you (Soul/God/Universe) expands toward the direction of your desire joyously. It's a shift in order to make your vibration equivalent to what you desire.

Why don't you have what you desire? Some People blame themselves most of the time. If they want something new, the actions required for the fulfillment of their desire is to fill the gap between **YOU (what you are now)** and **YOU (what you expect)**. What you currently are is your current frequency, and what you really want is your true frequency (peaceful, happy, and fulfilled state).When you appreciate what you have, and feel enthusiasm for life, you move in the direction of your natural state (Happiness & Peace). However, when you feel angry or resentful and focus on these feelings it results in failures because the source within you focuses on joy, love, and happiness, so it will never expand you towards your target.

Material and Spiritual are One

"We are Divine enough to ask and we are important enough to receive."
~Wayne Dyer

There are three stages of realization about your self are:

1. You are a sufferer (powerless). You don't have any control on life.

2. You realize you are in control of everything; you have power to visualize and take actions to achieve.

3. You are awakening. When you surrender to a greater power, miracles happen. You tend to let go and trust. At this stage you may realize you have a limited control. Gradually your connection with the universe strengthens. You have choice but no control. You live in constant state of astonishment and gratitude. Keep your ears open and listen to the whispers of the universe, which directs you toward the right direction. When the Universe whispers in your mind, it is called Intuition. Follow your intuition instantly. If something stops you from following your intuition then you need to clear your inner blockages.

You need to cleanse yourself throughout life because there is so much negativity in yourself and around. Keep cleaning and you will connect with the Universe more instantaneously and effectively.

Your Notes:

36

Aura
Your Invisible Energy Body

"The aura given out by a person or object is as much a part of them as their flesh."

~Lucian Freud

An energy field which originates from human beings and everything in the universe called **Aura**. There are **seven** layers of an aura. The outer layers are linked to soul, while inner layers are concerned with mind, emotions and health. Our thoughts, experiences and feelings affect the vibration of aura

Modern science has found that the human body is comprised of energy fields, which include electromagnetic, light, sound and heat fields. Moreover, few fields are received from outside while few are formed within the body. This process can be considered as **osmosis** between our and other people's energies because we absorb the energies of plants, animals, people, birds and everything in this universe. It's a sort of exchange of energies, give and take.

Aura is like a heat cloud emitting around people, shining with light and energy. It includes all imaginable colors, including those which are beyond the visible spectrum. We experience auras of other people during our daily life, but we ignore them most of the time. Mystics from all over the world speak about seeing lights around people. It's all about the recognition of the process, and we don't need to be mystic to see the aura. We should learn to see the aura, which requires understanding and patience.

Children are very good at seeing aura, they can experience the colors. Sometimes, they express it through their drawings. Aura surrounds the physical body and is three dimensional. It extends 8 to 10 feet around the body in all directions. People who have **strong** aura are less likely to be effected by auras of negative people, illnesses and negative outside forces. Those who are physically, emotionally and spiritually healthy are more vibrant and have higher energy; that's why their auras are healthy and strong. **Weak** aura fields are vulnerable to the outside influences, and people feel tired and low.

Aura is usually weakened by poor diet, lack of exercise, fresh air and lack of rest, stress, depression, alcohol, drugs, tobacco, negative thinking, show off and bad habits. It's an interesting fact that evil eye effects aura in a negative way. These days few people can't tolerate others when they are happy, successful, healthy, fit and peaceful. They invest their energies in destroying other person's happy relationship or good financial situation instead of improving their own. Sometimes their negative sigh, feeling bad and jealousy, curse can badly affect aura of people. There are many people who use black magic and their religious verses in negative way to hit other peoples' good stuff.

© Hina Hashmi

Features of an Aura

"The basic talent allowing us to see an aura is in all of us. In fact, we see auras all the time but are just not consciously aware of that."
~Mark Smith

We must understand the properties of aura to get more awareness and understanding about it.

1. All of us have **unique** energy fields, while there are some possibilities of similarities. Electromagnetic fields, light and sound are present in auras, but their strength and frequency may vary from individual to individual because every person has his/own frequency. Few people are closer to the frequency of our aura, and we feel good in their presence.

Similar aura patterns with someone indicate that we have same frequency at physical, mental, emotional and spiritual levels, while the opposite is true for the people whom we dislike instantly. We can feel agitation and a feeling of discomfort for the person whose aura doesn't match with ours. These subtle feelings reflect the extent of harmony that our aura has with the other people. It doesn't mean that the other person is wrong or bad; instead, it shows the difference between two individuals and their personalities. These differences can be resolved when people spend time with each other. We can learn to change our aura so that we can feel good with more positive people

2. Aura shapes itself according to the environment (e.g. if we spend time with positive people, our aura will be bright and bigger, while if we spend time with depressed people, we will feel drained because the energy always flows from a higher to lower concentration so that low vibration/depressed person will suck our energy and our aura

will be smaller).

We all are giving and absorbing energy constantly; whenever we come in contact with other people, there is exchange of energy. It exchanges more when you meet more people. We don't know about the debris, which we accumulate at the end of day due to our interactions with other people.

Sometimes, crazy feelings running in our head don't have something to do with our own self, but these can be due to the energy which we collect during the day. People who drain our energy are actually energy vampires, who leave you exhausted. Sometimes people feel some pain in our stomach or other parts of the body. This kind of exchange is considered unhealthy. Petting animals, spending time with plants and lowering our stress level impact our auras; these activities can lower our blood pressure, can balance our aura and stabilize our mental, physical and spiritual energies.

"Words were never invented to fully explain the peaceful aura that surrounds us when we are in communion with minds of the same thoughts."
~Eddie Myers

3. Auras leave imprints on the other people. People who are intimate and stay long with us have a greater and long-term impact on us. Specific kinds of energy patterns influence us when we are exposed to them for longer or even we can influence them. People with stronger energy can influence others .We magnetize objects and places due to the electromagnetic aspects of the aura.

If you sit on a particular sofa, your traces will be around that furniture. When your energy grows up in your room, you will feel the difference of feelings in your room and rooms of the other member of your family. Environment is charged with the energy pattern, which is harmonious to your pattern; that's why many people stay sleepless when they have to sleep somewhere other than their room. It takes time to adjust to new homes, beds, clothes, etc. because your aura needs time to harmonize the places and objects with your own frequency.

Your meditation and prayer blankets and shawls are magnetized with a specific kind of frequency of prayers. Every time you use them, they are more charged, and it becomes easier to access the meditative state of mind. The intimate exchange of energy (positive energy or debris) during sex lasts much longer than the usual contact. It's not easy to balance and cleanse that energy.

What do you think about the impact of energies on a foetus?
Do you think your child is a collection of your beliefs, aura, energy and thoughts?
Parents share auric energies with the children throughout their lives. The death of someone close creates a gap in the energies of other people who used to live with the dead one. People miss the energy they used to share with that person

"Someone's energy and aura and soul are so much more important -
they don't compare to what you have on."
~Rachel Roy

Colors and Aura

The vibration of the color that emits from our physical and **etheric** bodies expands 3-4 inches around the body. These colors change several times a day because they are influenced by the feelings and moods of an individual. One or two color vibrations remain constant, and these patterns are a reflection of a particular time span for months or a year. For example, the abundance of purple 5 to 7 feet around the body shows strong spiritual development for the past 6 months. Colors are a sort of barometer around the body that tell us the personality and general thought patterns of a person.

Here are what different aura colors can mean:

White – shows love, happiness, innocence and healing strength

Indigo- Artistic abilities and harmony with nature, self-control and mastery

Purple – denotes a strong spiritual attainment and character, wisdom, power, pride

Blue – shows someone is peaceful, intelligent and intuitive with a gift for healing

Green – hints material wealth, adaptability, versatility balance but can also be a sign of stress

Yellow – denotes love and kindness, optimism, compassion, while dark yellows show suspiciousness

Orange – shows energy and health, dynamic force, an ambitious nature

Red – indicates sexual power, physical life, lust and passion, also implies courage, strength and severity. Dark or cloudy red means violent or passionate energies.

Grey – denotes depression, fear, low energy and can reveal that someone feels trapped

Pink – shows a romantic, kind and good person, indicates presence self-love, modesty and high fertility

Black – can show past trauma and illness, evil intent

Gold – indicates highly spiritual, higher self, good qualities working with the divine

Brown – a down-to-earth, grounded personality but sometimes selfish.

How to Develop Healthy and Strong Aura

1. Take care of your nutritional needs

2. Recommended intake of water is 2-4 liters daily (depending on your location and season)

3. Do breathing exercise daily

4. Meditate for 15 minutes daily

5. Be thankful for what you have and offer prayers daily. Develop and strengthen your connection with the Universe/Divine.

6. Listen to and chant your religious mantras for maintaining good personal vibrations.

7. Be positive and careful about your intentions because your intentions and deeds always come back to you as events, circumstances, relations and experiences in your life.

8. Think about your own improvement/progress instead of affecting yourself and others negatively.

9. Exercise regularly.

10. Eliminate negativity including jealousy, revenge, comparison and competition

11. Please be careful while receiving energy treatments like Reiki, mesmerism and other types of touch healing or distant healing.

Be Aware of the Energy Treatments

These days many people do short courses and start practicing as healers. A lot of trainers certify people as healers for money hence serving the humanity becomes secondary for them.

Kind hearted people, including myself, are influenced by the attractive offers of these institutes. I was a master practitioner and trainer of Reiki but I suffered bad consequences. One of my Reiki trainers was cruel because he avoided giving **Reiki treatments** himself but he attuned and convinced other people to practice it. The worst thing he did was not telling others to beware of potential dangers which can affect the practitioners. I absorbed negativities of whom I used to treat and attune.

We share auras with people when we meet, talk and even think about them constantly. During Reiki sessions the universal energy flows through us in to the client and a connection is developed. If the client has negativities (illness, diseases, negative emotions, spiritual attacks) in his/her aura then those will be shared by the healer and vice versa during the energy exchange.

People aren't aware about the dangers of the exchange of energies because of the lack of education and because there are no immediate effects. Usually the after effects appear as weird physical sensations, illness and disease. Visiting a physician/GP is of no use.

I suffered six years of my life because my Reiki teachers were selfish. They didn't teach me about the consequences and the daily cleansing processes which are vital for a practitioner's safety and health. The spiritual (to heal the consequences of energy healing practices) treatment I went through was tough and frightening at times. The so called 'healers' I met were arrogant, cunning and selfish. They tried to keep me as a client for a long time and some tried to control my life as they wanted!

Please do not opt for a profession which involves energy exchange without exploring the details first. It can be dangerous for you more than anything. I know of many Reiki practitioners, including myself, who gained weight and had skin problems once they started treating people.

Even though the learners and practitioners have good intentions and they may be able to heal others but as we all know 'half knowledge is dangerous'. Many times I have asked God to forgive me because I, with incomplete knowledge, practiced energy healing.

In ancient times these methods were used by saints, yogi's and priests who had very pure intentions and they lived closer to the nature and knew all the aspects of this art. These days we live an unnatural life which includes: excessive use of electrical appliances, negative emotions, lack of connection with God and nature. Therefore it's difficult to stay clean and perform energy healing.

Be very careful while taking energy treatments even its distant healing. If you aren't sure about the positivity and expertise of your healer then don't make a deal.

Fact:

Showing off in marriage ceremonies and other events can create great troubles for us.

Most people aren't aware that sharing their photographs and other experiences on social media can have adverse effects. Photographs have our energy and auras in it, one sigh of jealousy or negative vibrations from those who can't see you happy or successful can disturb our auras. This can make our auras dirty and vulnerable to diseases, illnesses, spiritual attacks and negative vibrations. We must make sure that we share our achievements, beauty and good luck with our well wishers only otherwise one public photograph can change our life in an unbelievably negative way!

Chakras
Energy Centers in the Body

We are energetic beings and are comprised of love and intellect. Many times we feel powerless but always have unlimited energy within us. Our thoughts and feelings control the flow of energy around us. We have different energy centers in our body which are called **Chakras** pronounced as Chuck-raas (not shaak-raas as many do in the West).

As we have a physical anatomy, which is comprised of bones, skin, organs, muscles etc. we have an energetic anatomy which has three-dimensional arrangements of auras, chakras and meridians.

"In Indian metaphysical tradition and other belief systems chakras are points in the human body, i.e. major plexuses of arteries, veins and nerves, that are considered to be centers of life force or vital energy. Texts and teachings present different numbers of chakras. Their name derives from the Sanskrit word for "wheel" or "turning", but in yogic context a better translation of the word is 'vortex or whirlpool."
~Source: Wikipedia

These energy centres spin **clockwise**. Lower (related to the issues of material world) chakras spin at a lower rate while upper chakras (related to the Spiritual aspects) spin faster.

We have many chakras in our body but usually people know about a few which are next to the hormonal glands. Chakras, continuously, radiate energy. If we keep our mind full with negative thoughts then our chakras get dirty, slow, shrunk and dark. The malfunctioning of the chakras can create lethargy, lack of motivation, physical ailments and illnesses. Moreover, our intuition and natural capability to flow with life are disturbed.

"Each of these centres correlates to major nerve ganglia branching forth from the spinal column. In addition the Chakras also correlate to levels of consciousness, archetypal elements (Jungian concepts), and developmental stages of life, colours, sounds, body functions, and more."
~Bruce Sabalaskey

Chakras, our 'energy centres', play a vital role in our lives. So many diseases, illnesses and even psychological disorders are created due to the malfunctioning of chakras yet it's not a part of our education system not even taught at medical schools! The common man tries to deal with the problems with allopathic/drugs, which destroys our bodies in the long-run and the dis-ease prevails!

"Every organ, gland and body system is connected to a chakra and each chakra is connected to a colour vibrational frequency. For example, the heart chakra governs the thymus gland and it is also in charge of the functioning of the heart organ, lungs, bronchia system, lymph glands, secondary circulatory system, immune system as well as the arm and hands. And the heart chakra resonates to the colour green."
~Anodea Judith

These chakras operate **healthily** and perfectly when we have positive thoughts **full of love, happiness** and faith. They become vibrant, fast and radiant. We experience harmony in our lives and can experience peace and fulfilment. When chakras are balanced and cleansed we can access our **intuition** and our body works in a balance.

Eight major chakras are responsible for different functions in the body.

1. The Root Chakra:

It is located in the **base of the spine** (coccyx). Its Sanskrit name is *Muladhara* . It is **red** in color. When it is clean it looks like shining ruby while when it's dirty its color becomes muddy dark red. Its spinning rate is very low.

The corresponding organs for the Root Chakra are the adrenal glands and the sex organs. It is a centre of survival and self-preservation, general vitality, growth of infants and children. It can be linked with physical security, survival, material and the physical world too.

For example if we think about finances, career, safety, needs and our possessions then our thoughts (whether they are positive or negative) affect our Root Chakra. When we have fears about our physical requirements then this chakra shrinks in size, become dirty and dark. We must avoid worries about money, things or careers, otherwise it can disturb the working of the Root Chakra.

Imbalances of this chakra can create anemia, fatigue, cancer, growth problems, depression, lower back pain, frequent colds.

Physical exercise, yoga and deep sleep, consuming red food & drink, red clothing, bathing with red essential oils, etc. can improve the working of this chakra.

2. The Sacral Chakra:

The Sacral Chakra refers to the spleen chakra while it is called *Svadisthana* in Sanskrit. It is located **midway between your naval and the base of the spine**. It is a major entry point for air and it energizes the other chakras and the parts of the body. It has a beautiful shade of **orange** and it spins faster than the Root Chakra.

The Sacral Chakra connects with our sensing abilities. Its malfunctioning can cause low vitality, autoimmune disorders and blood ailments. The thoughts related to physical pleasures, e.g. sex, food, alcohol etc. affect this chakra. Moreover, our physical exercise, habits, weight and self-image link with it. Stress related to body issues, self-esteem, sex and food shrink this chakra and has negative effects on the working of this chakra.

The imbalance of this chakra can create eating disorders, alcohol and drug abuse, depression, lower back pain, allergies, yeast infections, urinary problems and sexual dysfunctions.

The stimulants, which can improve the working of this chakra, are hot aromatic baths, massage, embracing sensation, food and drink, which are orange in color ,orange clothing, using orange essential oils etc.

3. The Solar Plexus Chakra:

This chakra is **above the navel and in the stomach area**. Its corresponding organs are large and small intestine, pancreas (Islets of Langerhans that are groups of cells in the pancreas), the stomach, as well as the outer adrenal glands and the adrenal cortex.

The Solar Plexus is *Manipura* in **Sanskrit**. It appears in the shades of **yellow**. It spins faster than the other two lower chakras mentioned above. When it is clean and balanced it looks like bright sunshine. This chakra is linked with the heating and cooling of the body, power, control (a desire to be a powerful person, fear to be controlled by powerful people),balance of the intellect, self-confidence and humor. It acts as an energy-clearing house.

When people try to control others or they have fear that other people are trying to dominate or control them then this chakra shrinks and decrease in size and its working is disturbed. It becomes darker in color.

This chakra is the seat of lower emotions. The front part of this chakra governs expressed emotions (grief which makes you cry a lot) while the back governs suppressed emotions (long-held resentments). The disturbance in this chakra can also cause high cholesterol, hepatitis, digestion issues, ulcers, diabetes, nervousness, toxicity, heart ailments, parasites, colitis and poor memory along with many other diseases related to the organs this chakra affects.

You can read more self-development books, have proper intake of sunshine, do meditation and keep yourself relaxed to improve the working of this chakra. Detoxification programs, regular exercise and consuming yellow food and drink can be helpful.

I suffered from IBS & digestive issues for almost 8 years. This created great trouble for me because I always had a discomfort in my belly and stomach area. It affected my efficiency, mood, relationships and my daily life. I had medicines for many years. When I knew that imbalance chakras are one of the reasons for my trouble then I started putting efforts to learn and do chakra balancing. Afterwards I experienced a great difference in my health.

Few of my chakras have had higher energy levels. I realized that the flow of energy was blocked. I felt colder in the lower parts of my body. I identified that my lower three chakras had lots of stuck energy. It happened due to the extreme stress and an inactive lifestyle. I started doing yoga and breathing exercises, used magnets, did meditation regularly for the peace of mind. These actions created a great difference in my health. My digestion and body temperature issues were resolved.

4. The Heart Chakra:

Heart Chakra is the fourth major chakra in the body. Its Sanskrit name is *Anahata*.

The spiritual chakras relate to the *spiritual aspects* of the personality. While lower chakras deal with the *physical aspects*. It is located at the centre of the **chest at the sternum**. The corresponding organs are heart, lungs, thymus gland and circulatory system. The color of this chakra is a blend of beautiful **green and pink** but when it is dirty, it appears dark forest green.

This chakra is associated with relationships, love (all types including divine love, romantic and familial love), forgiveness (toward oneself, family, friends whether living or deceased, government, group of people etc.).

This chakra is helpful in the development of intuition because we feel love and pain through the Heart Chakra. It is the centre of worldly love as well as higher emotions. This chakra has connection with the solar plexus and the crown chakras. All kinds of fears related to relationships, love and forgiveness, compassion, ability to have self-control, and acceptance of oneself can shrink and darken the chakra that badly affects it's working.

The malfunctioning of this chakra can cause heart and circulatory ailments, lung ailments, chest pain, high blood pressure, passivity and immune system problems.

Its working improves by spending time in nature, doing forgiveness regularly for others and oneself, spending quality time with family and friends.

5. The Throat Chakra:

The Throat Chakra is located in the **centre of the throat**. Its Sanskrit name is *Visuddha*. It energizes and controls the throat, thyroid and parathyroid glands. It has a correspondence with the Sacral Chakra because the Throat Chakra is the higher centre for the creativity while the sacral chakra is the lower centre of creativity.

Its spinning speed is faster than the lower chakras and its color is **sky blue**.

This chakra is associated with being true to you as well as with other people, singing, speaking, artistic tasks, and teaching other people.

The disturbance in throat chakra can cause goiter, sore throat, loss of voice, asthma, thyroid imbalances, fevers and flu, mouth, jaw, tongue, neck and shoulders problems, hyperactivity, hormonal disorders such as PMS, mood swings, bloating and menopausal issues.

6. The Brow or Third Eye Chakra:

The Third Eye Chakra is located in the **centre of the forehead** at the hairline and regulates the nervous system, directs the life force throughout the body. Its Sanskrit name is *Ajna*. It's colour is **Indigo**.

It is used for clairvoyance and intuition development/sensing; trusting one's intuition and insights; developing one's psychic abilities and self-realization; releasing hidden and repressed negative thoughts.

It records everything that has happened in your life including everything that you think, feel and do. A deep indigo surrounds this chakra. It is affected by your thoughts (worries and fears) related to your past and future.

The disturbance in this chakra can cause loss of memory, paralysis, epilepsy, learning disabilities, co-ordination problems and sleep disorders.

7. The Crown Chakra:

The Crown Chakra is located at the **top of the head** and controls and energizes the brain and the pineal gland. Its Sanskrit name is *Sahasrara*. It has a vivid royal **purple** color. This chakra is associated to the concept of God & religion, learning about spirituality and Divine Guidance. This chakra is responsible for integrating one's consciousness and sub consciousness into the super consciousness.

When the Crown Chakra clogs with unhealthy emotions about Divine Guidance and religious beliefs, it looks dark as the sky at night.

Disturbances to the Crown Chakra relates to issues with the pineal gland and the brain whether these are physical or psychological in nature, headaches, photosensitivity, mental illness, neuralgia, senility, epilepsy and even skin rashes.

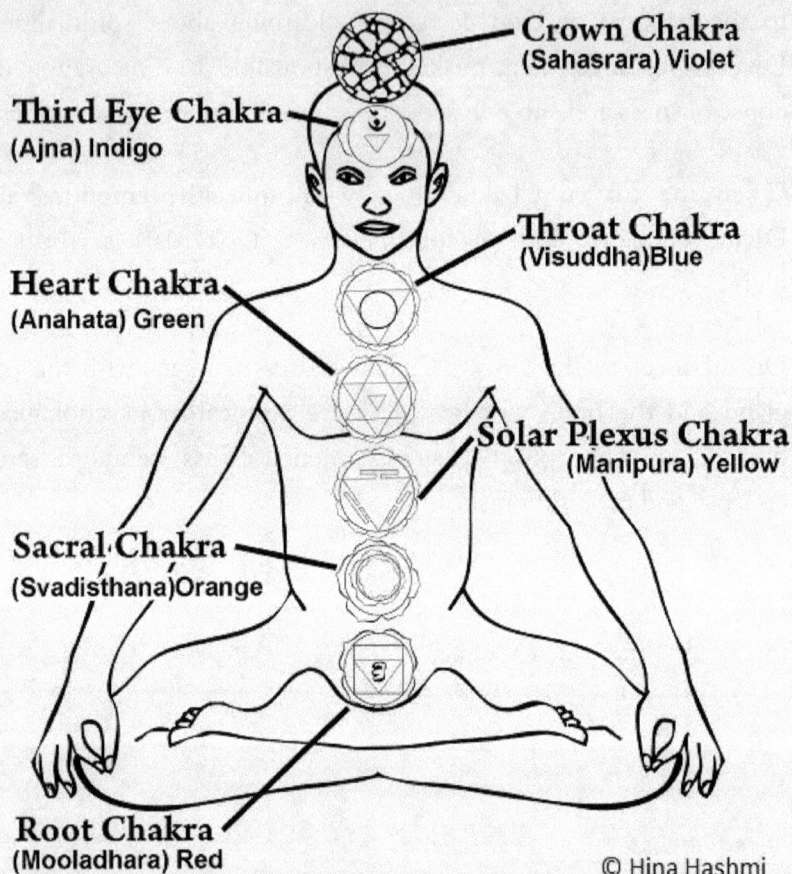

Crown Chakra
(Sahasrara) Violet

Third Eye Chakra
(Ajna) Indigo

Throat Chakra
(Visuddha)Blue

Heart Chakra
(Anahata) Green

Solar Plexus Chakra
(Manipura) Yellow

Sacral Chakra
(Svadisthana)Orange

Root Chakra
(Mooladhara) Red

© Hina Hashmi

Keeping Your Chakras Balanced:

When we have multiple fears and worries about anything in life, whether it is about relationships, money, careers, etc. these can cause our chakras to shrink. On the other hand, when we have obsessions our chakras can inflate too. If all the chakras are of different sizes then this can disturb their balance, causing us to become unwell, either physically or mentally; and can even cause spiritual unrest.

Therefore, a healthy mind, body and spirit is when all the chakras working efficiently and are of equal sizes.

There are many techniques for the balancing and cleansing of the chakras. Here are a few steps that we must follow to have healthy and balanced chakras.

1. Regular **exercise** helps to maintain balance of chakras whether it is a walk, aerobics or jogging because it releases the blocked energy in the body.

2. Regular **yoga** and breathing exercises help in balancing the flow of energy and keeping the chakras aligned.

3. Daily **meditation** for 15 to 20mins daily.

4. **Positive mind-set** is most essential factor to keep our chakras work healthily. All kinds of fears, worries, doubts, obsessions and negative emotions obstruct the working of chakras.

5. We must learn to **forgive** people regularly. Forgiveness releases us from the prison of hatred, revenge and repentance.

Your Notes:

Laws Of The Universe
Learn the Working of the Universe

"As you simplify your life, the laws of the universe will be simpler;
solitude will not be solitude, poverty will not be poverty, nor weakness."
~Henry David Thoreau

There are few rules on which this universe is based, which are called **laws of the universe** (people may call it God, divine or higher power). We are designed to function according to these laws. Most of the people are unaware of these laws, and they believe that life is all about collecting material wealth, power and fame. They make relationships on the basis of money and other benefits. Some people want to prove they are superior and their actions are based on jealousy and competition. They don't experience contentment and happiness. Understanding of certain laws and loving/compassionate support of each other is required to create a better life for one and all. Positive, truthful and helping people always get rewards. Oneness, love, compassion and enlightenment can be attained by following the spiritual laws of the universe. We need to be our own guide. We can live a much more peaceful and happy life if we think about positive growth of ourselves and others, and its effects on the universe. The ego (selfishness) must be withdrawn, and life must be lived peacefully. Human beings always have free will, whether they follow the laws or not.

As Within, So Without

"As above, so below. As within, so without."
~The Emerald Tablet, circa 3000BC

Life gives us many opportunities to learn about ourselves. Lessons are presented to us through our outside world, because it's a reflection of our inner world.

Suppressed anger has a potential to attract more angry people into our life. They will serve as a mirror for what we have denied. If you have a deep sense of abandonment, people will reflect that back to you. They may leave you or withdraw emotionally. Self-criticism and negative thoughts about yourself will attract people who reflect this back to you, showing critical behavior and can abuse you physically. Selfish and negative individuals pay the price until they learn their lessons.

"When you love yourself and are happy, you will definitely have loving people around you. Your surroundings reflect how you think about yourself. The purpose of challenges in your life is to wake you up, get you on the track which leads you towards the purpose of your soul. Positive beliefs about yourself pull generous-hearted and honest people in to your life."
~Hina Hashmi

The person who feels secure, loved, safe and happy inside will have a secure, safe and happy life. Your inner integrity will be matched by those around you.

This law applies even to the physical body. Our bodies are reflective of our inner feelings. If we feel emotionally or sexually vulnerable inside, we may build a protective layer of fat over our abdomen or hips, the places where we hold our emotions and sexuality.

"I always say, when the voice and the vision on the inside become more profound, clear and loud than the opinions on the outside, you've mastered your life."
~Dr John Demartini

The Law of Request

"Whatsoever ye shall ask in prayer, believing, ye shall receive."
~Matthew 21:22

Asking is essential according to the spiritual laws. You must ask for help if you really need it. Some challenges in our lives are actually a part of our learning process .When we rush for help without asking, we create obstacles in the learning. Some people continue with their old unhelpful patterns even if someone helps them (when they have not asked for any help). When we force our help on others we bear the negative effects of karma, if it goes wrong. Don't rush to offer help. If it is uninvited it is bad manners and most probably will not be acknowledged or appreciated. Sometimes people create their own mess due to choices in their lives. The universe wants them to face challenges. You comfort the sick and bereaved, but that sickness or bereavement was part of the plan to help that person grow. However, in many cases, if you feel upset by the mess someone has gotten themselves into, it is your stuff. It is an indication that you need to look at yourself rather than rescue someone else.

My friend's grandmother was miserable and wasn't ready to have a social life or ready to meet new people after the death of her husband. My friend kept trying to convince her to go out and make new connections but she wasn't convinced or ready to do so. The solution to this problem is, "when she is ready, she will ask for help". The response of my friend's grandma could be a projection of my friend's issue i.e. her reluctance to meet new people or she feels rejected when someone doesn't accept her help.

My aunt's issue was her desperation about her daughter's marriage. She refused to marry anyone and she was afraid she'll never get married. How can my aunt help her? The answer is: When her daughter will break her own fears she will be ready. Perhaps she knows at some deep inner level that she won't find the right man for herself. Maybe she knows it upsets my aunt and this is her way of punishing her. She could have a million reasons. However, she is clearly serving her mother by bringing up some of her stuff. I suggested to my aunt, "Unless she asks you for help, stop trying to help her and look at what it means to you".

There are times when it is appropriate to ask for help. By asking, I do not mean screaming with frustration like a toddler, or crying like a victim who doesn't want to take any responsibility for his/her actions. By asking, I mean carefully assessing the situation and then calmly, and with strength, requesting the help you need. Remember the answer lies in the question. The more clarity you have in your question, the better quality of help you will receive.

"People who ask confidently get more than those who are hesitant and uncertain. When you've figured out what you want to ask for, do it with certainty, boldness and confidence."
~Jack Canfield

The Law of Attraction

*"The simplest way for me to look at the Law of Attraction is if I think
of myself as a magnet, and I know that a magnet will attract to it."*
~John Assaraf

Universe serves as a mirror to us. People around us play a very
important role in our lives. We usually deny that we didn't attract
certain kind of situations and people around us. Universe wants us to
look in to our shadows but the negative aspect of our personality
denies that fact. (This law is explained in detail in Section No.3)

If someone's unmarried partner doesn't commit to a relationship,
he/she must look inside and work on his/her fears related to
commitment. When these fears and limiting beliefs are resolved, the
partner will either leave him/her or will commit. How can a happy
person have depressed people around him? People are attracted to
mirror our inner-feelings. They serve a purpose in our lives.

A couple contacted m because they were desperate to have a baby
but the woman couldn't conceive. They had tried almost everything.
No apparent reason for why they could not conceive was found. A
soul was waiting to enter in to their life and I told them that their
anxiousness is blocking his arrival. The couple surrendered and tried
to make their life happy without a child. A great energy shift took
place and they sent the vibration of contentment out, which allowed
that soul to enter in to their lives. Sometimes people are desperate at
a subtle level which blocks their marriage or other relationships.

A bossy kind of man who just wants to dominate will definitely
attract a woman who will let her to be dominated. It isn't something
that is planned, instead it is unconscious. An empowered and

stronger woman cannot be in a relationship with such a person, unless there is some lesson to be learned from being in such a relationship.

The Law of Attraction works on many levels. When we chose to be loving, compassionate and open, we get the right person in our lives. It's all about our beliefs. If you believe no one is like minded and people don't understand you, then they won't. You will get people around you who will not understand you because you attracted them. Remind yourself of your good qualities and attract someone who appreciates you. And, of course, there are cases where the opposite poles attract.

The Law of Resistance

"What is needed, rather than running away or controlling or suppressing or any other resistance is understanding fear; that means, watch it, learn about it, and come directly into contact with it. We are to learn about fear, not how to escape from it."
~Jiddu Krishnamurti

Focus can always bring things closer to us. People, material and situation come in to our lives because of our thoughts and beliefs. When we don't want those experiences, we try to push them away. When we use our vital energy in resisting what we don't want, we attract more of it whether it's a person, circumstance or challenge.

Once I had a belief, which disturbed me before my job interview that the interviewer would ask difficult questions and will be harsh. I was very fearful and repeatedly thought about this fear many times before my interview. So what happened? It did become the most difficult interview I had ever been to. The power of strong resistance created that bad experience during the interview. Usually people are unaware of the **law of resistance** and yet they use it all the time!

Your conscious mind has the ability to understand the difference between positive and negative instructions, while your subconscious mind isn't capable of this differentiation. Even when you are busy and involved in a task and, simultaneously, someone is talking to you about something else; your unconscious mind will take those messages in. Resistance of illness will cause illness. Repeating positive statements can program your mind to think in a positive way. Avoid **worrying and negative thinking** while you are relaxed because at that time your fears may manifest!

'Don't', 'can't', 'won't'… this kind of words call upon the law of resistance. Your thought about not ever finding a perfect job will resist the best opportunity for you. Anything you are resisting is around you as a thought form. One good way of dissolving thought form is to write down your fears and burn them, then write what you really want in life and start visualizing it.

"The Universe never asked you to struggle. It is simply answering your mood."
~Abraham-Hicks

The Law of Attachment

"Renew, release, let go. Yesterday's gone. There's nothing you can do to bring it back. You can't "should've" done something. You can only DO something. Renew yourself. Release that attachment. Today is a new day!"
~Steve Maraboli

Attachment is defined as **conditional love**, while love with the universe is eternal and unconditional. If you want someone to behave according to your rules then that's not love, that's attachment. You can release these bindings in multiple ways. Don't expect too much from others because people behave according to their perspective, not yours. Accept people as they are and avoid controlling them, only then they will give you their best. Forgiveness is required to dissolve all these negative cords because it releases shame, guilt, anger, hatred, etc. When you forgive yourself, you free yourself from memories which aren't serving you anymore. Detachment is a basic requirement for seeking enlightenment. Anyone or anything we are attached to his power to manipulate us although we all have freedom to choose.

The Law of Attention

"The moment one gives close attention to anything, even a blade of grass it becomes a mysterious, awesome, indescribably magnificent world in itself."
~Henry Miller

This law of attention is exact. We manifest with the attention, irrespective of whether it's something big or small. Attention denotes **focus** on our thoughts, feelings and actions. When we don't concentrate on something, quarks disappear. Quarks are the sub atomic particles which are created by focused thought, and now can be filmed. Our expectations(positive focus with 100% belief) can change our life.

Tom was organizing a workshop for stress management and had little expectation that it would be filled, while Katy was organizing a small event but she had higher expectations that seats will be filled. Both of them got the results they expected. Katy sold all the seats for her event, while Tom got fifty percent attendance for his workshop. Katy met her targets due to her clear vision and positive attention towards it. Doubts and fears are obstacles which stop us from manifesting our dreams. It depends how much we focus on the positive outcome. Positive Focus and desired results are directly proportional.

The Law of Flow

"If you want to find the secrets of the universe, think in terms of energy, frequency and vibration."
~Nikola Tesla

This law governs all areas of our life. This universe is a like a river of **flowing energy**. We all are connected and everything is moving. When the flow of a river is blocked, it overflows or breaks the barriers. Similarly, emotions can also over flow when their expression is blocked. This blockage affects relationships, uncontrolled emotions are frightening for other people, so they avoid coming close to interact or make relationships with such people. A peaceful river is attractive for many people; similarly peaceful emotions are attractive for other people to connect with you. You must carefully notice your emotions and their effect on your relationships.

To buy something new, to attract nice people in your life or to replace home furniture; you have to replace the old stuff, whether it's clothes, old thinking pattern and beliefs, or people. According to this law every new thing/people/circumstances require space to enter in to your life. Use this law to change your life according to your desires.

The Law of Abundance

"Abundance is not something we acquire. It is something we tune into."
~Wayne Dyer

The Universe has gifted us with **abundance** of everything, whether it's love, happiness or prosperity. Abundance means a **flow** of everything and it's our birth right. The big obstacle which blocks us from receiving abundance is our own consciousness. Abundance is always available to us, while our limiting /negative thoughts, emotions, beliefs and memories are a barrier for us. (Explained in detail in the next few pages) .

If a parasitic plant surrounds a tree which produces fruit, we cannot consider that plant abundant because parasite will not let it grow. It's a gardener's duty to remove the parasitic plant around the fruit producing plant. In the same way you must remove all the beliefs and thoughts which inhibit the abundance flowing in to your life.

People block abundance of love by closing their hearts, growing weeds, like fears and rejection, around their hearts. That's why they are stuck in relationships or become withdrawn. Success is not about exerting force on something because that can cause frustration and worthlessness. Abundance is about going with the flow and enjoying your journey while benefiting from it Universe gives us what we want when it knows that we are capable of taking care of the gift. For example a toddler's parents don't gift him/her a precious toy until they know that he/she can take care of it properly.

Whatever you desire, start doing it for others. You want more friends, be friendly with people. Release the blocks which stop the flow of friendliness like hurt, suspicion and jealousy. Abundance consciousness will direct the flow of material wealth in to your life.

The Law of Prosperity

"This is the law of prosperity. When apparent adversity comes, be not cast down by it, but make the best of it, and always look forward for better things, for conditions more prosperous."
~Trine, Ralph Waldo

The Universe is like a **loving parent** who wants us to have everything we need. Claim your power and be prosperous. A wrong mind-set is like bad soil that restricts a plant's growth. Similarly, limiting beliefs about 'what we deserve' hinder our growth. They stop us from being abundant in every area of our life. Deservingness is very important to attract prosperity in your life. The Universe is like a huge pool in which all resources are available, and we draw according to our consciousness and positive mind-set. People with a poverty mind-set remain poor and usually it is because of the fears in their mind. They tie up energy in the lack of money, and some people think God doesn't like rich people.

Greed is also bad because it's like unassimilated food in our system. If we eat more than our body requires, it will lead us to indigestion. Stubborn people and people with low vibrations don't feel contentment and happiness because they have a poverty consciousness. In contrast people who have prosperity consciousness and they apply it in their lives are open minded, content, happy and generous.

The Law of Intention

"A purpose, an intention, a design, strikes everywhere even the careless, the most stupid thinker."
~David Hume

Good Intentions bring success in everything you do. Intention is always supported by universal energy because it's a base for manifestation.

Intention is a powerful force in motion. When you throw it into the universe it starts working for you; like an archer who pulls his bow back and grasps it with intention because he aims at his target before setting it free.

Clear positive intention helps in overcoming all obstacles, and success is assured. Few people just *'hope'* to meet their targets, while few have clear and strong intention and they do it. Intentions are more powerful than 'wishes' and 'hope', because force released from intentions makes things happen.

Karma is like a balance sheet of out deeds and thoughts. Assessment of our karma depends upon our intentions. If your car hit an old lady and she is hurt, would you be responsible? Well, if you are in your senses, and tried your level best to save her, then you aren't responsible. In contrast if you are drunk or careless then you will bear karma for this action. On spiritual and/or physical level you will have to pay for that action. It can be in any form and cannot be predicted. This accident could have happened to teach you a lesson.

We must be careful where our intentions are coming from, is it our ego's desire or in the highest good of every one.

Evil intentions create a black mark on your soul, whether you did something bad or not, intention has been sent to the universe as a vibration and been noted. Some People feel frustrated even when they have clear and positive intention because nothing good happens to them. One of the reasons why their manifestation is delayed could be that the Universe wants them to learn some lessons which are essential for their growth and happiness in the long run.

The Law of Manifestation

"When you concentrate your energy purposely on the future possibility that you aspire to realize, your energy is passed on to it and makes it attracted to you with a force stronger than the one you directed towards it."
~Stephen Richard

Until now, unknowingly, you have used various laws of the universe like; attention, attraction and prayer, to manifest whatever you have in your life right now. If you want to manifest something then you must be clear about what do you want and how to increase you vibration. Then your desires will manifesting the physical reality. When you desire to have a loving, open and sincere friend, you must develop these qualities in your own personality beforehand.

The power of manifestation is great but you must intend to manifest which is in the highest good of everyone. That's why it's essential to meditate and listen to your intuition. Ask for what your intuition has guided you for and then visualize what you want because visualization is the strongest tool for manifestation. Writing your desires down can be beneficial if you don't feel comfortable visualizing.

Hold your vision firmly in your mind. If you want a job then visualize its manifestation and be positive about it. A detailed written description will give information to your left brain which is your logical mind. Relaxation and repeated visualization will bring synchronicity between the right (creative mind) and left brain. You must have qualities matching to your desires. Focus on the feeling of satisfaction within your dream job. Bring the thoughts of your inner feelings of satisfaction into your mind, which will align you with your desired job offer. Do regular meditation while holding the vision of your desire and also take necessary action in the direction of your desire. How to attract/manifest is explained later in this book.

"Personal satisfaction is the most important ingredient of success."
~Denis Waitley

The Law of Success

Universal energy always supports free will. Success is usually defined by achieving whatever you want at the material level. You can use the **law of attention** to achieve material success whether this is for good or bad. You can't afford to have a single negative thought if you are determined to achieve something.

Be clear about what you want, have strong faith and put all your efforts into achieving your target. There is an energy of beliefs which vibrates around you. You must get rid of those beliefs which create a hindrance to your success. Beliefs like **'I am loveable'**, **'I am generous'**; attract happy and peaceful relationships in our lives.

You must always speak what you believe and walk your talk. This attitude will make you successful in the long run. When people want success but visualize failure, they attract failure because they don't know about the power of pictures. Pictures are much more powerful than thoughts. When two aspects of you fight with each other, the outcome can be depression, frustration or exhaustion. If success arrives unexpectedly, that indicates your good karma that helped you fulfill your desires.

Few people have evil intentions like cheating, hurting or cursing, while some people help others and work for the highest good of everyone. Surprisingly, sometimes, negative people are more successful, which feels discouraging to the positive people. People with negative intentions may be successful, but they have a lot of karmic debt which they have to pay during their life time and when they have challenges, they think that they are trapped by bad luck. There are many people who earn millions but are not happy within and/or feel unfulfilled. This shows that they are failure emotionally and spiritually. They earned material success which didn't give them happiness.

If a business man harms multiple lives during the process of being successful, then he cannot be considered as successful. Good deeds move you towards the right place, at the right time, and with the right people. When you succeed in good things, ultimately you will experience enlightenment/ascension.

The Law of Karma

"Karma, a word that translates simply as action, is an ancient believe that every action has a consequence. Good and bad karma are the results of good and bad actions."
~Dr Synthia Andrews

We always get rewarded for our deeds - **'as you give so you receive'**. When we send kindness, love or happiness, into the universe, we get back the equivalent or more of it and if we send anger, hatred or jealousy we get it back in some form or other, this is called the law of Karma.

Karma is always recorded and balanced throughout our lives. All positive thoughts, emotions, words and actions are credit while negative ones are debit. The negative energies when sent out in the universe will reap an equivalent (or more) of that. It can come back as health problems, an accident, material loss or painful relationships.

One of my clients Lisa always believed that universe would take care of her. Moreover she believed in kindness, optimism and integrity, and was a very loving and happy person. She experienced a big loss in her business and had to sell her house. Soon after that she met with a car accident but she didn't change her belief that universe always takes care of her. Suddenly she received a £750,000 cheque from an old neighbor whom she took care of a few years back. She told me that she always got support throughout her life.

Wonderful things happen due to positive beliefs and good karma. Change your mind set to earn good karma and make your life beautiful. Change those beliefs which no longer serve you.

"I'm a true believer in karma. You get what you give, whether it's bad or good."
~Sandra bullock

Every time you throw a thought in the universe, it changes the state of your vibrations. When you help someone then don't expect equivalent favour or support back from that person. Reward can come through unexpected sources at any time.

Examine your state of vibration

(Thoughts + feelings + Actions) $\xrightarrow{\text{Affect}}$ *Different areas of life*

The Vacuum Law of Prosperity

"Nature abhors a vacuum. And since the inherent nature of the universe is good, a vacuum will always be filled with good. So, one of the fastest ways to manifest prosperity in your life is to create vacuums."
~Randy Gage

If we want great things to happen then we must create space for what we desire.

The Spirit always expresses itself perfectly. It's not essential to hold on to something to know it. Our spirit requires freedom in every area of our lives. The barriers that stop our soul from free expression are doubt, guilt, resentment, and thoughts of lack or limitation. These ideas block the flow of creative energy from and to us. We require space for the beautiful image we hold in our mind. We can create space for what we desire by letting go of all obstructions. Visualize your body as an instrument, through which creative energy flows.

Explore Yourself:

In the space provided below; make a list of the areas in your physical world in which you need to create a vacuum. If you want new clothes, furniture, or anything, you must have a space for it. Create space for the things you desire for example you must create some space in your wardrobe for new desired dresses. If you need loving people in your life then you must get rid of selfish and negative people.

Beside each area, write a date/deadline to create the space for what you desire.

AREA	COMPLETION DATE
_____	_____
_____	_____
_____	_____
_____	_____
_____	_____
_____	_____
_____	_____

The Law of Compensation

Sowing and **reaping** doesn't exist at the same time. You should do your best while sowing, nourishing, and protecting because this effort will give you a high quality crop. Your efforts today will be rewarded but there is no assurance of when it would happen .It can be sooner or later than our expectations. So we must have patience and faith, and wait for the best returns.

"This law of perfect justice and fair compensation permeates the activities of humankind whether we know it or not, whether we see it or not. Every day is a day of judgment, for every day of our life we are reaping the harvest we have previously sown, whether good or bad. And the law guarantees that in the long run every virtue is rewarded, every wrong is redressed – in silence, in certainty, in Divine order."
~Emmet Fox

The Law of Vibration

"No one can deny you or grant you anything. It all comes to you by virtue of your vibration."
~Esther Hicks

This law states that everything is in continuous vibration and motion. Inertia doesn't exist. Make your vibration harmonious with your target. **Frequency is defined as the rate of vibration**. Energy is neither created nor destroyed. Everything is merely in a constant state of change, being manifested in all varying degrees of vibrations. We have the marvellous power of co-creation and we can change vibrations according to our choice. If you are repeating negative thoughts like "I am not feeling good", the results you get will be similar to what you repeat.

Conscious vibrations travel through the subconscious mind to the body. If you have knowledge and understanding of vibrations then you can change them instantly. **Ignorance** leads to **worry** and doubt. Most of us don't know how to control our inner vibrations which can be effected by the events in the outer world.

The state of worry or doubt can cause mental illnesses. When you impress worry in the subconscious mind, an emotional state appears which is called 'fear'. That fear energy expresses itself through the physical body. Your body experiences vibrations of anxiety which can lead to an illness or disease leading to death.

Understanding vibrations helps us in making decision for building positive circumstances inside instead of outside.

Types Of Mind and their Relation To Body

The Power of the Human Mind

"The empires of the future are the empires of the mind."
~Winston Churchill

The human mind is a spectacularly miraculous thing. It is a human mind—your mind— reading these words right now. If you are reading these words in a building (for instance: your home, office, or A library), human minds created it. Minds conceived it, and lots of human minds (and bodies) worked together and built it.

The human mind also created science ,religion, philosophy, mathematics, history, and every work of art that has ever existed. Here are just a few things your miraculous mind can do: analyze, brainstorm, create, dream, engineer, form, generate, have a hunch, imagine, judge, know, look forward to, meditate, originate, plan ,rationalize, speculate, think, understand, visualize, and wonder.

The human mind is an awesome factory for the realizations of dreams. It's clear that if you plant a desire it becomes a reality but there are some conditions and the most essential one is the faith in your dream. Blend this faith with positive beliefs, appropriate actions, positive thinking and emotions. Then you will be on the right frequency of materialization of your dreams.

The Super Conscious Mind

"The Super Conscious is sometimes referred to as the "collective unconscious."
~Carl Jung.

This mind is fearless and has no restrictions. It's considered as a **collective unconscious** and has a higher purpose. It has memory of everything during all the times when you acted in full awareness as a divine being. All your natural talents and capabilities originate from here (e.g., love, joy, peace and happiness, etc.) Even your intuition resides in your super conscious mind. You experience direct knowing (intuition) through this mind.

The Conscious mind

Man is the most powerful creature on the earth because he can decide what he allows to enter his conscious mind. Nothing can force him to pick up negative (low vibration) ideas. Conscious mind has the power to select information.

Any thought or information first of all enters in the conscious mind and its role is to accept or reject any idea. Human beings always have a choice of choosing their thoughts. Nothing can force us to pick any memory, circumstance or relationship without our permission. You become what you think about.

"The conscious mind may be compared to a fountain playing in the sun and falling back into the great subterranean pool of subconscious from which it rises."
~Sigmund Freud

The Subconscious Mind

This part of the brain is a **subordinate** of the conscious mind and it functions in every cell of the body.

The sub conscious mind doesn't have capability of rejecting what your conscious mind has chosen. Whatever you think again and again affects your feelings and is impressed upon subconscious mind and becomes a part of your personality. Once these thoughts are fixed as ideas they don't need any conscious assistance, they express themselves often until they aren't replaced. These ideas become beliefs and habits.

> *"The subconscious mind gathers information through emotional input."*
> ~Bob Proctor

Your Body

"Take care of your body. It's the only place you have to live."
~Jim Rohn

Body is the **house** in which you live. Actually, it is the **smallest** and most obvious part of us because it's just an instrument of the mind. The body is the physical presentation of us or, the material medium. Our body moves in to action by the thoughts selected by our conscious mind and then impressed upon the subconscious mind. Subconscious mind exists in every cell of the body. Our results are determined by our actions in which you are involved.

Thoughts

↓

Feelings

↓

Actions

↓

Results

To change the results change your thoughts!

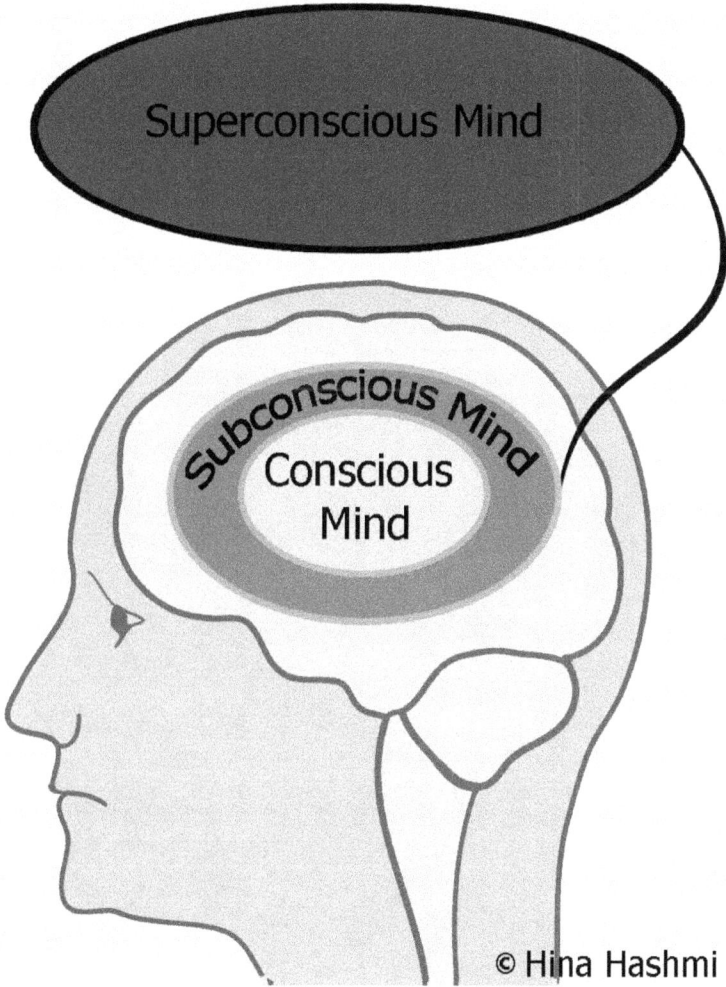

Superconscious Mind

Subconscious Mind

Conscious Mind

© Hina Hashmi

Your Notes:

SECTION NO: 2

Listen to your being. It is continuously giving you hints; it is a still, small voice. It does not shout at you, that is true. And if you are a little silent you will start feeling your way.

~Osho

Emotions
What Your Feelings are Trying to Tell You?

Human Beings are Sensitive to Vibrations

"One individual who lives and vibrates to the energy of pure love and reverence .For all of life will counterbalance the negativity of 750,000 individuals who. Calibrate at the lower weakening levels. "
~Dr. Wayne Dyer

We are all human beings and are sensitive to vibrations. When mother conceives a child these few cells formed from embryo vibrate and the mother's heart beat effects the vibration of fetus's heart. Most important factors are mother's emotions, habits, behavior and tone of her voice which imprint on the fetus hormonally. When the infant is born he possesses the instinct of his parents. So parents must keep a new born close to heart. His heart gets stimulated with the heart of parents and mind gets message that he is safe. This heart to heart connection is essential for growth and survival.

According to Goleman (Author, Psychologist, and Science journalist) children are highly empathetic. Sometimes they think that they are a source of disturbance in the home environment, when they see any close one in pain. This is a characteristic of human beings to consider themselves responsible for their circumstances. Sensitivity and empathy are basic tendencies of human beings.

We all are naturally highly sensitive, intuitive, visionary and designed to spend spiritual lives. But our society is superficial, materialistic and has too many rules to live by. Our schools teach mathematics and statistics but nothing about how to spend a happy life. We are programming our children to be insensitive. Gradually we are becoming insensitive to the vibrations of others.

On the other side there are some people who can use this information about vibrations at the right time and take proper actions accordingly. They are very sensitive hence they can feel and learn about the spiritual dimensions and can communicate with spiritual beings. Our sensitivity is always working whether we are aware or unaware of it.

When a child is born he develops subliminal systems for feeling things and for feeling habits. It's all about behavior, habits, thought patterns and reactions of the people around the child. It depends upon the response which a baby receives, whether this system becomes open, radiant or self-protected.

We usually react according to the information saved within our subliminal level. We are usually unaware about our subconscious and unconscious sensitivities. Very Few people can control their feelings without getting trapped in the information their sensors gather from the environment they are in.

Think about a child; a small vibrational being who didn't learn words and a coping system. He was whole love and joy. A healthy childhood is marked by this kind of soul validation but when his parents emitted signals of fear and mistrust; he felt rejected. The experience of outer world entered in his life and it left negative impact on him from that day. That's not his real and true self. A set of rules developed by his father wasn't a choice of his soul.

He defines himself as a specific kind of a person according to the rules of his parents and society. In short he doesn't allow energy to flow through him abundantly. The fast vibrations and energy which come from the universe are unfamiliar to him because his body is habitual of conditional love and acceptance. This vibration doesn't match with his original vibes and he feels threatened, overwhelmed and fearful. This is a story of many kids and adults (grown up kids) around us.

When energy penetrates in our body the mental blocks(explained in the next section) cannot be suppressed any more. Our main task is to make adjustments with those vibrations. We need to become a pure love channel and change these contracted feeling habits. It's not an overnight task. It's actually a process of unlearning and new learning which requires patience, repetition and perseverance. Be ready for your soul's renewal as it was at the time of your birth.

"When you offer a vibration, the Universal forces are working in concert with each other in order to satisfy you. You really are the center of the Universe. Abraham."
~Esther Hicks

Characteristic of the People with Mental Blocks

- People develop **phobias** and don't want to face their troubles.
- They don't have a room in their relationships
- face troubles in job.
- They feel lost, depressed, disoriented and have memory loss.
- They avoid facing problems so they use distractions like alcohol, drugs, food, exercise, shopping, worrying or internet.
- They don't live in the reality. They chose thinking and talking about celebrities, non-physical things or past lives; they develop over-dependent relationships in which they don't care about their needs.
- They prefer to take care of an ill relative than taking care of themselves.
- Losses in business or problematic situations in their personal lives.
- They feel helpless, exhaustive and drained.
- Moreover people feel unlucky and have bad health.

"Our entire lives are created from our emotional (feeling) state. This is the powerful energy that creates our reality. Everything that shows up in our outer world is a direct match with our Emotional Belief Systems."
~Melanie Tonia Evans

Actions Based on Positive Emotions

"By choosing your thoughts, and by selecting which emotion al currents you will release and which you will reinforce, you determine the quality of your Light. You determine the effects that you will have upon others, and the nature of the experiences of your life."
~Gary Zukav

- People provide space to other people without forcing their opinions/beliefs on others.

- They are aware of the frequencies of other people and don't match their vibration with the ones who have low vibrations.

- People with positive feeling habits take control of their frequencies; they merge with new peoples' frequencies, seek knowledge and come back at their own vibration and decide whether to implement this knowledge or not.

- They tune their body to the vibration which nourishes most at the present moment.

- They always look inside themselves and try to get messages and sensations and feelings.

- Moreover they are excited about their connection with the world and are highly creative.

Explore Yourself:

Make a list of the negative emotions which you experience often.

1. Identify the why's of those emotions.
2. Forgive people, situations and yourself for creating these emotions.
3. Stop when you notice yourself indulging in a negative emotion.
4. If you fight with somebody who doesn't understand your point then stop yourself, calm down, re-centre yourself and try to understand his/her paradigm.
5. Don't punish yourself. Just try to create positive emotions.

Your Notes:

Your Emotions and Negative Vibrations

Few experiences in life affect us at a deeper level. Negative experiences lower our personal vibrations and we feel bad. This state attracts more negative experiences leading to negative vibrations. Lower vibes are bad for health of the soul. People usually get stuck in negative vibrations which hinder their success. When growth is complete for one phase, we learn new lessons and it's time to move on to the next level. When we don't realize our lessons and prefer to stay in our comfort zone, we stay stuck in the same phase.

Some people are very rigid with job security. The universe gives them messages to move on but they keep fulfilling their needs for certainty and security. Our life moves in a cycle of construction and destruction. Ideas and phases; come, we implement, and then we let go. All of us are trying to get desired results before the time which universe decides for us. We don't try to understand the mechanism of the universe.

If we continuously protest and complain about our life then we actually create barriers in the manifestation process and the natural flow of life.

One must avoid getting stuck in the negative memories because these can block personal growth. Our subconscious mind just follows our previous reaction to the same kind of experiences. This can result in punishment, control, anger and blame. Focusing on the things which we couldn't achieve will result in nothing but waste of time & energy.

"The Universe does not know whether the vibration that you're offering is because of something you're observing or something you're remembering or something that you are imagining. It just receives the vibration and answers it with things that match it."

~Abraham/Esther Hicks

Value Behind Emotional Reactions

We were born with the sensitive and sophisticated translators of vibrations which we called our five basic senses. Whatever we see, hear, smell or taste are actually the vibrational interpretations of our senses. Emotions can be understood by our every vibrational content. Emotions serve as our guiding system. They tell us what we feel about something. This indicates the degree of alignment with the source's energy. We can learn gradually when we allow source energy to flow through us at a higher level. All emotions fall in to range of high frequency emotions to low frequency emotions e.g. joy to disempowerment.

"To experience positive emotions you don't need a big house or a nice car or a managerial job or a million dollar in your bank."
~Maddy Malhotra

Positive thoughts are a source of joy, love and an indication of our alignment with source. Negative thoughts create disharmony in our body for example depression, fear and aggression indicate misalignment with the source. When we give our attention to what we don't want, we, unconsciously, attract more of it. Our attention creates reality.

"Every intention sets energy into motion whether you are conscious of it or not."
~Gary Zukav

Negative Emotions are not Your Fault

"Right now and right now and right now and right now everybody has a mood or a feeling. Even if you don't even know that you have it, right now you all have a mood or feeling, and That mood or feeling is causing you to send off, or put out a vibration. And how many kinds are there? Two. And they're negative vibrations and positive vibrations. So that means right. Now, whether you all like it or not, or understand it or not, you are all emitting or putting off this vibration. There are only two kinds: negative or positive."
~Michael Losier

Let's start from the childhood. Behind every negative emotion was the misunderstanding of energy and life. You don't need to blame yourself because while these emotions were developed you didn't even know how to speak.

You aren't perfect. You can always choose to adopt the path of your soul (explained in Section 2)You can be love-full anytime. You just need to identify the reason behind the feelings you experience. It's easy to unlearn any feeling habit. It's in your control. Decide on developing a positive feeling habit today otherwise you would stay stuck in a vicious loop of negative feeling habits. If you want a positive and happy life then stop feeling self-pity or seeking attention for your problems and take action towards creating a positive and fulfilling life.

You have two options whether to speed up or block your soul's intentions. You have a choice: to act out of **selfish ego** or as a **loving soul.** When you choose being a loving soul, and give proper attention to your dreams without using your own will power, then you are in a process of creating a range of experiences which flow into your life harmoniously. Then you feel pleasure in everything in your life. After dissolution of fears, your mind and emotions act in harmony to help you to make you a joyous soul. You don't need to do extra efforts to get what you desire. Every essential and light thing will show up for you.

Detecting Positive Emotions

"At the end of the day it's not 'what looks good' that matters, it's 'what feels' good."
~Maddy Malhotra

When you are thinking about something general, your vibrations are very small and don't have a power to pull experiences, things or people. Automatically the same kind of vibrations will join those small ones. When your thoughts get momentum, you tend to notice your feelings. When those feelings are same as your true frequency, you experience a range of positive emotions and vice-versa.

Your feelings show your level of alignment with the universe. Feeling good indicates you are allowing what you have desired for. As you know, emotions are A set point for attraction. So whenever someone appreciates you, you feel good and your vibrations have high amplitude. When you face criticism, your reactions would be just the opposite. People conclude beliefs from the experiences and develop emotions related to that.

A child, who has seen his parents fighting and found them in pain, is vulnerable to instability in his personality, especially in his future relationships. Whenever he would think about marriage, he would experience anger, rejection, and hopelessness. When parents discuss fear of some disease using an example of some close one's death, children can develop a fear of that disease and develop an emotional set point of physical vulnerability.

Good news is that these set points are always under our control. Thoughts like weeds will grow automatically unless we train them according to our choice. Thoughts gravitate according to what's happening around us. We develop a feeling response according to what we observe. Gradually, we feel powerless about life. We always have control on these set points and we can change them when we want. Our vibrational essence will be same as our emotional set points, which are created by thoughts.

"Happier thoughts lead to essentially a happier biochemistry a happier, healthier body. Negative thoughts and stress have been shown to seriously degrade the body and the functioning of the brain, because it's our thoughts and emotions that are continuously reassembling, reorganizing, re-creating our body."
~Dr. John Hageli

Mental Blocks

A Barrier to Personal and Spiritual Growth

How would I materialize my dreams? This one question is very disturbing for most of us. While exploring this question people develop many inner-blocks e.g. fears, doubts etc.

These are blocks within you whether you are aware of this fact or not. If you experience any emotion like frustration, hesitation or anger, while planning your dream life, means you need to clear some blocks. Also, allow the universe to play its part to help you manifest what you want. Whenever you experience any block **affirm** in your mind "I know what I want is on the way to me, it just hasn't arrived yet. I deserve it".

Joe Vitale (Author, Speaker and Law of attraction expert) enlists **seven** limiting beliefs that we can encounter:

1. I am not good enough to be loved.

2. No matter what I do, I should be doing something else.

3. If it hasn't happened yet, it never will.

4. I don't know what I want.

5. I upset people.

6. I better stop wanting because if I get my hopes high, I shall get hurt.

7. If I fail I will feel bad for a long time and will be too scared for the next attempt.

Beliefs Create our Reality

Beliefs are the **repetitive thoughts** of a person. Disturbed cognitions are actually the **irrational beliefs** which are easily accessible below the surface of consciousness. Irrational beliefs are core beliefs which affect many important emotional and behavioral functions. Usually they stop people attracting what they want. One way to identify your beliefs regarding anything; finances, relationships or career, is to look at how you feel about people who are already successful in those areas. If you feel good and can easily visualize yourself possessing those things then your beliefs are in alignment with the manifestation process and you may need less work doing on your mind-set. However, if you feel any negative emotion and your inner voice tells you that you cannot have it or you do not deserve it then you need to do a lot of work on clearing your blocks and creating new self-beliefs.

Every human being has a threshold of deservingness within himself. The main task is to identify those limiting self-beliefs, dissolve them and replace them with new empowering beliefs.

Positive change in a belief can impact multiple areas of life. It doesn't matter how many times you repeat affirmations for success but if you don't change your core beliefs, the changes will be temporary.

"The beliefs/blueprints which were created in the first few years of your life (when you didn't even have the ability to question what your mind was recording) are still there and affecting your feelings, attitudes, decisions and actions every day."
~Maddy Malhotra

Beliefs were Thoughts Once

Your thoughts exist. Whatever you have thought today, yesterday or many years back, it is energy and it exists. Your attention activates thoughts and it is strengthened with your effort. When you want something to move out of your life, pull your attention out of that. Give attention to what you want. If you are worried about your health and keep thinking how bad it is then change it and start thinking about possessing a healthy body and finding ways to make it better. Gradually your vibration will become strong.

When you continuously give attention to a positive thought, it becomes a **dominant** thought. While practicing this thought again and again it becomes a bigger part of your vibration.

Doubt is one of the most dangerous **negative** vibrations and can ruin the materialization process. When you have strong desire and strong doubt, these two vibrations cancel each other.

If you really want to do, be or have anything, then destroy your greatest enemy 'doubt' first. The manifestation of your desire is directly proportional to how much you believe.

The main source of doubt is your limiting beliefs!

"If you don't have the successful career or business that provides the money, fulfillment and freedom, the loving and joyful relationships you desire, the ideal body shape or weight, high self-esteem or self confidence, it's all because of your beliefs!"
~ How to Build Self-Esteem and Be Confident: Overcome Fears, Break Habits, Be Successful and Happy by Maddy Malhotra

Limiting Beliefs

Limiting beliefs are the repeated negative voices in your head. Your thoughts which consist of negative beliefs send out negative vibration. When you think **'I am not good enough'**, this thought vibrates back in the form of situations which prove that you aren't good enough.

Explore Yourself :

Identification of Limiting Beliefs:

You can identify limiting beliefs in your words and sentences. For example:

Desire: I would like to be fit and should like to have a slender body.

Belief: I can't because I am fat genetically.

Desire: I would like to have a loving life partner

Belief: I can't have one because I don't deserve it.

How to Deal with Limiting Beliefs:

You can change your beliefs by creating new statements for yourself. Following are the steps to write your statement:

1.Find out if someone else has already achieved what you want to achieve.

2.If yes, then how many people can you think of (or find out) who have achieved it

3.Now write your statement but as a third person (see example below).

4.Ensure your statement is believable.

Example of Limiting Belief:

I would love to attain my ideal weight but I can't because obesity is hereditary.

Q: Do you know anyone who has a body weight different to that of their family members?

A: Yes

Q: If so, then how many people can you think of who have or had this?

Allowing Statement:

Some have a different body shape than their family. I can see many people in my city, work place and even I have example of my friends.

You need to find out the doubts from your desired statement. You can feel it if you give attention to the little voice inside you. Write these statements in general terms because their relation to you can cause more doubt.

Your Notes:

Explore Yourself :

1. Write down the practical applications of your limiting beliefs with accompanying emotions and behaviors?
2. Make a list of your beliefs regarding different areas of your life? For example finances (money doesn't come easily or rich people are bad).
3. Are these beliefs helpful in your life?
4. If you continue to think this way or feel this way, what will be their effects on your life?
5. What are the logical reasons of following these beliefs? Maybe you will find many reasons, but when a belief is irrational it will be logically unsupportable.
6. Do you have a proof /evidence for the support of your belief? Are any religious and authentic sources in favor of your beliefs?

This exercise will serve as a revelation because if you strongly believe that nobody loves you then this belief is affecting your life in a negative way. Usually irrational beliefs don't have any kind of logic or support from any kind of authentic text.

Explore Yourself :

Make a list of the real advantages and disadvantages of changing your irrational thoughts and beliefs. It's essential to keep yourself aware of the reasons on the basis of which you have decided to change.

Explore Yourself :

1. Write down the details of a real situation which provoked unpleasant emotions?

2. What were your streams of thoughts then and what memories or other details can you recollect regarding the situation?

3. Specify the emotions which you experienced during an event and give it a rating. For example if you experienced anger, rate the intensity by giving rating between 1 and 100. Higher the intensity, higher will be the rating like 85 or 90 or whatever.

4. Write down the automatic thoughts which preceded those emotions?

5. Identify one belief working behind those thoughts. For example if someone believes that 'I am not good enough' can result in thoughts like :

- I don't deserve a great life
- Nobody loves me
- I cannot be successful ever

6. You have to find out the belief working behind many automatic thoughts.

Your Notes:

Your Notes:

How Life Works

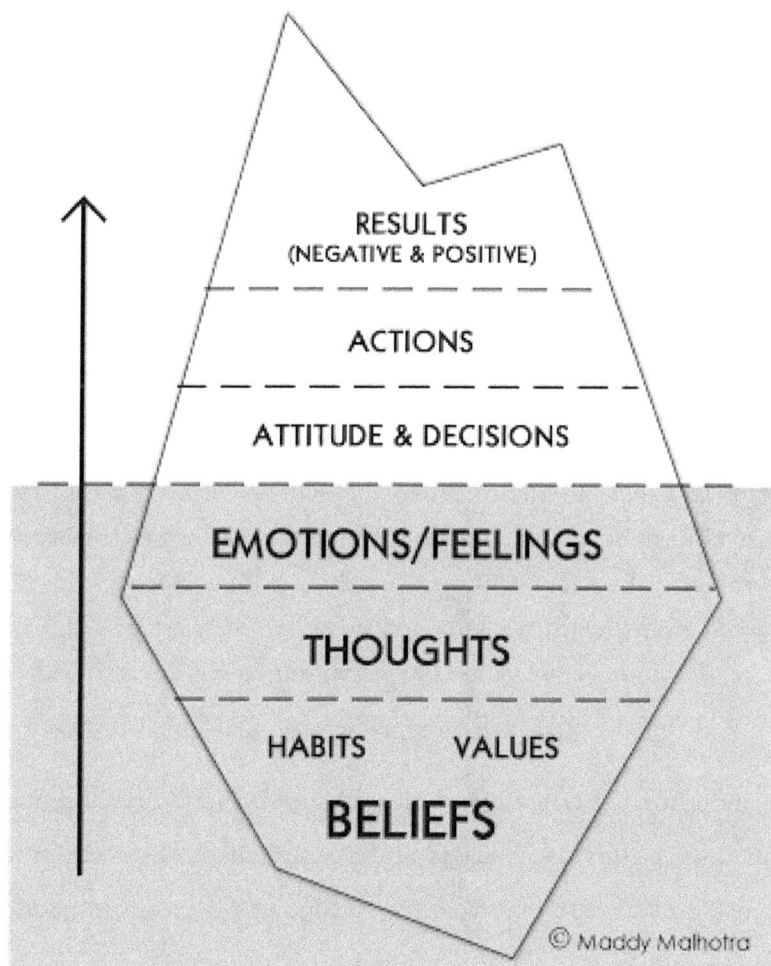

RESULTS
(NEGATIVE & POSITIVE)

ACTIONS

ATTITUDE & DECISIONS

EMOTIONS/FEELINGS

THOUGHTS

HABITS   VALUES

BELIEFS

© Maddy Malhotra

How to Resolve Mental Blocks?

Thoughts and feelings are two of the most important forces that shape our lives. These forces work at the unconscious level, while information influences the subconscious mind. You will have to program yourself at the subconscious level.

Sometimes, people think that nothing seems to work including the law of attraction. It happens due to the blocks in their minds. These blocks can be removed by working on their beliefs.

Ask your unconscious mind about the beliefs which aren't good for you, it will give you the right information, and then work on those beliefs.

This is an excellent way to attain the state of effortlessness. These blocks stop us from taking action. When we take action, our actions become effortless at one stage. Initially, a corner block in the mind prevents a person from taking action. When we start working from our heart passionately, all the blocks within us will be resolved. The actions become effortless at that stage.

The indicators of our **alignment** with the universe are: absence of limitations, positive self-beliefs and positive memories in the mind. When the blocks are removed, the outside world comes in harmony with our intentions. If we don't work on releasing these block we cannot access intuition and flow with the life.

Two things are important to accomplish your dreams:

1. Clear your inspiration.

2. Take steps in that direction.

You can measure deservingness by asking yourself this:

How well can you spend your life?

You see, everything going on in your life is stemming within you. The control of your life should always be in your hands. What other people (family, friends, and neighbors) think about you should not stop you from moving forward in life.

Life has no meaning. You give meaning to everything. Your beliefs influence the meanings you give. Your judgment about situations is based on the beliefs you hold.

One positive person affects the whole universe. If you improve yourself as human being then you will contribute for the betterment of the whole planet.

Zero Limits:

Spiritual Mind (SP M) Super Conscious

(I M) Conscious Mind

(E M) Subconscious

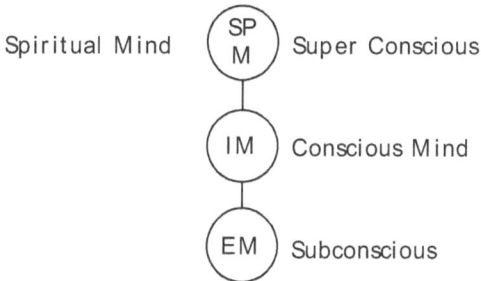

The process of Ho'oponopono was developed by Dr. Hew Len Ihaleakala. According to this approach, when you forgive people, events and circumstances, you are in the process of change, which leads you towards your final destination, love.

Toxic energies are replaced with healthy, positive energies. Love starts flowing by occupying the minds; starting with the spiritual mind (the super conscious), then flows through the intellectual mind (the conscious mind) freeing it of thinking energies and finally moves into the emotional mind (the subconscious) where thoughts of toxic emotions are eradicated by it. We all want to beat a place where we are one with our desires. At this place, no memories, events or beliefs can affect our intentions. We are one with the Universe/Father/Mother/God/Divinity/Source (whatever you may call It).

At this point, whatever you desire, you can manifest unlike, most of the time, when we are fighting with the blocks within us. There are limits in current reality; by dissolving those limits, you connect with the source (nothingness/blankness).

In every moment, you make decisions based on a memory (a belief or a limitation within you) or inspiration which comes to you directly from the desire.

You need to clear memories. Memories are thoughts, beliefs, feelings, your past, and programming from media, schooling, parents, friends and what we watch on television (the movies). Where is the pure spirit within us? Usually, it's covered by the nest of irrational beliefs and unhealthy emotions.

Great goals always come from **inspiration**. One of our duties on this planet is to dissolve the negative emotions associated with negative memories while we motivate ourselves and other people.

"Everything I am doing in my life is coming from a memory. Memory is the virus of the mind that has attached itself to your brain."
~Anon

There is a sense of detachment in the clearing process. If you repeat four phrases:

1. I am sorry
2. Thank you
3. Please forgive me
4. I love you

Repeat these phrases while thinking about the Universe/God; moreover feel the connection with it while chanting. Keep dissolving the effect of the negative memories. When you dissolve memories, you are at the place that is very close to zero, closer to the Divine.

When you are close to divine and get intuition from divine, life becomes easy. It's almost like your guardian angels making a way for you. When you dissolve negativities, the divinity can live through you. Intuition is where peace, magic and glory are. It all goes back to your phrases. You can pray to the divine, who knows the best ways for healing your thoughts and memories that are holding you back.

Beliefs are the determinant of experiences. If you have beliefs which oppose your desires then you will end up not getting what you want.

The divine is sending you and other people ideas every moment.

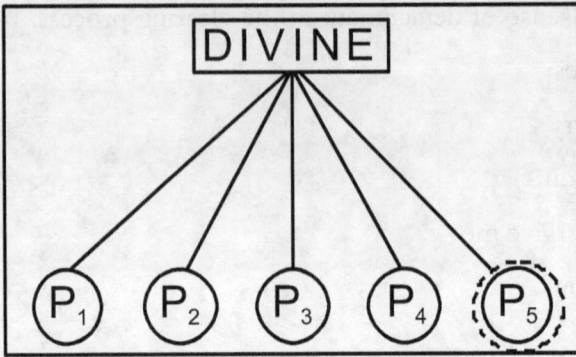

P1, P2, P3 and P4 are the people who are unable to catch the idea because of their intentions and belief system.

Only P5 is the person who is open for divine's message, and he gets the benefits.

Working of the Universe

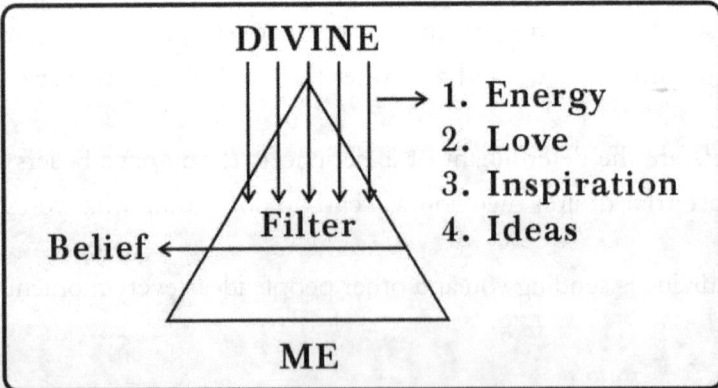

Belief can create blocks.If you don't believe in divine; you stop the divine.

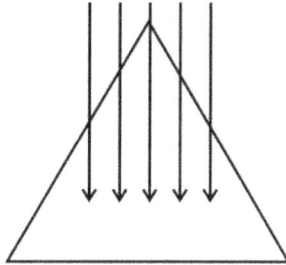

Erase the middle block

DIVINE

ME

Your Notes:

Intuition
Discovering the Voice of your Spirit

"This word 'intuition' is beautiful. You know the other word, 'tuition'; tuition means somebody else is giving it to you. Intuition means nobody is giving it to you; it is growing within yourself. And because it is not given to you by somebody else, it cannot be put into words."
~Osho

The main purpose of your life is the alignment with the consciousness. Your real self always tries to guide you whenever you emit low vibrations. The Universe always speaks to us and provides guidance. We need to be focused and present to listen to the messages we receive. These messages and guidance, we receive from the Universe are called **Intuition**.

If we are too busy with daily tasks and/or our mind is full of worries/negative thoughts then we can't access intuition. When we don't focus on internal nudges then we get some signals, from the Universe, in the form of life events. For example, we will get sick and experience obstacles while completing our tasks. Most of the time, we behave according to the labels given by others. If we have identified ourselves as a "workaholic" or a "Best performer", then our conscious mind neglects intuition regarding relaxation, physical health or relationships.

We must learn to identify the difference between intuition and conscious thoughts. When we do not get a break, from daily routines, for a long time then how can we expect to go with the flow?

"Intuition is always right in at least two important ways; it is always in response to something. It always has your best interest at heart."
~Gavin de Becke

We get inner guidance Through the Super Conscious domain while the subconscious domain represents the working of our subconscious mind. Our soul expands itself to get new energy and information through collective unconscious. The **collective unconscious**, originally defined by Carl Jung, refers to a segment of the deepest unconscious mind. As opposed to the personal unconscious, which is composed of long-forgotten memories and experiences, the collective unconscious consists of archetypes that represent an inherited set of beliefs and understandings collective consciousness has lot more information than our own inner self".

The human body is able to perform one task at a time. When we chose to connect with the super conscious domain, we focus on doing one task at a time with full concentration and dedication and when we are connected to the subconscious domain, we try to do many tasks at one time. We always have a choice to select the domain with which we want to connect. We must operate our lives from the super conscious domain because our soul knows what's best for us in the bigger picture.

My friend Elizabeth is a business owner. She sets goals when she starts her day and then connects with the higher self by being silent and calming her mind. Then, she starts her day. If she has ten tasks, the order of the tasks is set according to the intuition she receives and she follows the guidelines received. That's why she completes every task easily. After every task she calm herself down, takes a deep breath, and allows her soul to guide her. Happiness and fulfillment are the outcomes which she experiences often. She tells me that life, people, circumstances and situations support her most of the time.

"Listen to your intuition. It will tell you everything you need to know."
~Anthony D'Angelo

Explore Yourself :

1. When you have a pain or disease in a part of your body then with a calm mind close your eyes, centre yourself and focus on that part of your body.

2. Ask your intuition to guide you about the incident, thought or carelessness which caused it. You can get answers in variety of ways through dreams, precognition, poetry, sign board, song or book.
3. Apologize to your body that you didn't care for it.
4. Now, send lots of love to that organ or part. Let it heal itself and you will see the effects of this positivity and love in your life.

Healing isn't an overnight process, it takes time. Choose to release the false reality and return to your real self.

People are so conditioned to repeat behaviors/habits that they cannot act upon their intuition. When intuition tells that it's time to switch over career, very few people take action. Most of the people aren't ready to take any risks. If someone who has earned money in the construction business then how can he decide to quit and become an artist? Actually that's the point where one should follow the guidance from the soul/universe/Go/Higher self. By being stuck in our conscious mind, we block the way towards peace, happiness and fulfillment.

Your Notes:

Train your Intuition : This Voice Inside will Guide You What to Say and What to Do.

Listen to the Voice of the Soul

People spend most of their time in finding faults and discussing others. As a result, they cannot get insights and instructions about their body from their soul. Your soul is the part which is connected to the **Higher Self**. We miss the messages when we aren't attentive. Our mind automatically takes over and we don't listen to it. Most of us keep focusing on negative feelings and habits. Letting go of the past and negative feelings and moving on with the time is the best strategy to connect with the higher self. We must avoid sticking on to negative people, relationships or beliefs which aren't good for us. Life isn't static, it's flowing. So we should flow with it.

We learn by our experiences and use them to decide what's better for us. Every individual has a different personality. Few people learn from other people's experiences and others learn from betrayal, losses, cheatings, and disasters. Few learn by being creative. There are some who never learn and keep blaming others.

Every individual has different needs. Every image that appears in your mind has a purpose. Maybe for the resolution of old negative memories or traumas. Some images can warn us about future losses and profits. Our inner voice/guidance is our best friend. It tells us everything and is our best companion.

Human spirits want freedom of creativity and expression. If your intuition wants you to write something, then be creative. Otherwise it will go to sleep. Intuition becomes part of your life when you seek connection with the divinity. Bring some changes in your daily routine, change the sequence of your daily rituals.

"If you choose according to your own inclination and according to your own intuition, it is very strong in children but, slowly, becomes weaker. The voices of the parents and the teachers, the society and the priest, become louder and louder. Now if you want to find out what is your voice, you will have to pass through a crowd of noises."
~Osho

Learn to Let Go

Most people think that their prayers must be answered instantly. We must wait for the response of the universe calmly and patiently. We don't follow the above process when we are frustrated, fearful or worried.

When you feel stuck remember that you are a part of the life wave that is always moving. This may be a time for new turns in your life. Just relax and allow yourself to be a part of the flow and realize that everything and everyone is a part of the same flow. It's required to transform yourself into a positive vibrant soul.

"If prayer is you talking to God, then intuition is God talking to you."
~ Wayne Dyer

Now make a list of those ideas which are higher on the scale and those ideas that allow your intuition to flow and act on them.

Your Notes:

Benefits of Following the Super Conscious Mind

"The secret, or innermost, level of wisdom is pure intuition, clarity, lucidity, innate wakefulness, presence, and recognition of reality. This transcendental wisdom is within all of us—it just needs to be discovered and developed, unfolded and actualized."
~Lama Surya

Sometimes you think that your suffering is worse than everyone else is, but actually, this is not true. This type of thinking shows that you are in a kind of self-imposed hypnosis in which you are the victim. You re-affirm to yourself that you are unlucky. That's why you experience painful and negative events. The crux to changing your story is that "You are 100% love and that's your real identity." When you allow your body to live in the super conscious domain, you actually free it from self-pity and fear.

Explore Yourself:

1.Write down your mental, emotional and physical weaknesses from your subconscious domain.
2.Write down your feelings and views about the times of pain, betrayals or loss of loved ones.
What were the messages behind them?
The Universe was trying to teach you something for you to move forward, what was that?
3.Write down your achievements during this process of change/enlightenment?
4.If this process has completed then what kind of steps would you like to take right now as an enlightened person?

Your Notes:

You aren't Alone

"The only real valuable thing is intuition."
~Albert Einstein

Soul has some presence in your body; it's around you and a part of every atom in the universe.

There is a **wiser one** who accepts you as you are, provides you with whatever you want and witnesses all your life experiences. People call it God/the Universe/Higher self/Almighty/Divine/Source etc. Imagine he loves you the most. You can call him a best friend. When you know he is within you and with you, then it becomes easy to get connected and listen to the messages which he conveys continuously.

We continuously communicate with him so open your eyes, ears and mind to listen to what he communicates with you and shows you the right way. Practice it frequently and you will feel the divine within yourself. Make friends with everything you notice. You may be surprised how much guidance you receive when you believe in the wisdom of the world. You should learn to live in the present moment and feel everything around you to connect with the universe.

Be Open to Receive Super Conscious Guidance

"Do not assume that divine guidance flows only when you are in need of help. Guidance continues to flow whether or not you have problems. It transcends problems, heartbreaks, and traumas, flowing through dreams and illuminations. Whether guidance comes during times of tranquility or trauma, however, it is up to you to have the courage to acknowledge it."
~Caroline Myss

People, usually, develop guilt for their past events. The best way to get relief from this painful feeling is to develop a new paradigm. We must develop a skill for understanding the context of the events from the super conscious' view. The path of intuition requires acceptance and openness so we can accept the truth about ourselves. These truths can come from within us as well as from outside.

Guidance from the super conscious is always available to us, regardless of age and time. When our conscious mind doesn't understand the message of the super conscious then the divinity can use a friend, a sign board, a dialogue in the movie or books to guide us. You can also be a source of guidance for others.

Steps to Obtain Guidance for Life:

1. Deep Breathing and Relaxation:
Acquire deep relaxation by smoothly breathing in and out for a few minutes. Feel yourself completely safe.

2. Feel the Presence of the Higher Self:
Allow all kinds of emotions in your body whether positive or negative. You must stop thinking about your needs. Just feel the presence of the higher self within yourself.

3. Feel Your Connection:
You need to bring your body, mind and spirit in a perfect balance. You are connected to the divine through your head. Feel from the base of your spine that you are connected to the earth. Energy is flowing through you from the top to bottom.

4. Your Identity:
You are a part of the higher self. Your body is your identity and a tool to carry your spirit. Reaffirm in your mind that you are unlimited energy. Let the real voice speak within yourself. Allow your thoughts to flow with the natural flow of life. Feel the connection with the whole universe.

5. State Your Questions:

Try to state your question more specifically because incomplete/unspecific questions will not bring the best answers.

6. Ask for What You Desire:

Now connect with the higher self and ask what you desire with a firm belief that you will get the perfect answer.

7. Be Receptive and have Faith:

Now trust that highest power who knows what is best for you. Send your request without any doubt.

8. Allow and Trust the Inflow:

Shut up your judgmental mind. Be open for the ways of receiving and final form of the answer. Avoid refinement of the answer. Expect the unexpected.

9. Keep Your Eyes and Mind Open to Recognize the Answer:

The Source may use various mediums to convey your answer. You may receive it through pictures, words, precognitions or symbols. The answer can be revealed in the inner or outer world. It can be conveyed by both living and dead. Now this is your responsibility, to decide the appropriateness of the answer according to anxiety or truth signals which your body generates after receiving the answer.

10. Feel Gratitude and Implement:

You must be thankful for the awareness of the intuition on different levels of consciousness. You must appreciate your body which always cooperates with you. Now take a step towards implementing the information you received.

If you still aren't sure about the intuition received and have doubts, then do this small exercise to clear the doubts:

Explore Yourself:

Imagine an open place in the nature where you are alone. Now visualize a huge hall made of crystals, move towards it and feel the frequency of the crystal. When you and the hall are on the same vibration you will be able to enter it. You have to feel more positive to be able to enter in to it. The environment inside is very clean and mirrors your soul. Now sit down on the floor and feel connected with the earth, sky and heavens. Be assured that no one can enter in to your space because nobody has the same frequency as you. The visions you receive will be of the highest vibration. You need to create a pull to attract answers and it will be done by the feeling of desire, need and incompleteness. You must be very specific in your questions to the super conscious so you get the best answers. If you want to get married, ask first, 'Will I get married?' It shouldn't be where, when and how initially. Then ask other questions gradually. Maybe there are a few lessons which you need to learn. Ask how you are subconsciously blocking experiences in your life? Only the source can give you the perfect results. Believe that your presence on the earth has some purpose.

Explore Yourself :

1. Write or imagine your questions about your need? Now decide how would you like to release them in the universe? Would you like to write it on a piece of paper and let it fly away with the wind? Or would you like to place it in an imaginary balloon which can take it away?

2. Be ready to receive any answers.

3. Now relax and stay open for the answers. Don't try to modify the answer in any way. Answers can come in a variety of ways as mentioned earlier. Once you get it, express gratitude and say out loud that you have got it. Gratitude will open your heart and deepen your connection with the source.

Your Notes:

Seeking Inner Guidance

"Listen to your inner voice. For it is a deep and powerful source of wisdom, beauty and truth, ever flowing through you. Learn to trust it, trust your intuition, and in good time, answers to all you seek to know will come, and the path will open before you."

~Caroline Joy

The inner world is much deeper and more powerful than the flat conscious mind. Dreams can act as a pathway towards the truth. When you experience dreams, you are alive and a part of them. Use them wisely. Don't take them for granted.

You can give new questions to your conscious mind which will be picked up by the super conscious mind. Re-dream your dreams while you are awake. Do it in your imagination. Especially relive your horrifying/frustrating/painful dreams. Introduce new characters which will be there to help you out. All these fears, horror and resistance have always been created by your own mind.

Know Other's Through Your Inner Guidance

Your body is a great machine which is composed of energy particles. Everyone is in the **unified field** of energy and information is transferred in the form of vibrations. If you just use your imagination to know the details of someone, you can get the right insights by using this method. You can know about your friend on four aspects.

1. Current situation
2. Limiting Beliefs
3. Actions required
4. Results of these actions

Explore Yourself:

Sit down, take a few deep breaths and relax. Imagine your friend sitting in front of you and your body is collecting impressions in the form of symbols. Understand and interpret those symbols. You may get all the required information.

Explore Yourself :

1. List five major issues of your life in a hierarchy of their intensity.
2. Imagine you are highly intuitive. What does your intuition tell you about those issues?

Your Notes:

Personal Force for Manifestation : Using just Will Power isn't Enough for Manifestation

When you want to materialize something out of your fear, ego and stubbornness then your desires takes control of your life. You use your own force without harmony. The overextended energy will stop you until you let yourself flow with love and faith. When you want excessive money out of greed, with much effort, it can materialize but it may not last long and you will have to pay a big price for it sooner or later. Inner-joy, love and peace will disappear from your life without a doubt.

Once you understand the law of attraction you will know that nothing is separate, what's going on outside is linked to your inner reality. Every thought in your mind has a potential to become an event in your life. Every event, every thought and every emotion can educate you. Get yourself synchronized with the higher self.

Trust the Flow of life

"God's spirit is able to flow through us as we minister and teach others. You just never know what God is going to do with the people he has placed in your life."
~ Allen Bach

The wave of life provides you the opportunity to let go of the old patterns and opt for new options. Your task is to trust the wisdom of the universe. Go with the river of energy wherever it goes. Sometimes, it flows over the stones, sometimes you need to be calm and do nothing, while sometimes action attains results.

I tortured myself for many years by using extensive, personal force to get significance from family, society and relatives. I ran after obtaining degrees, one after the other, so the society and family respect and praise me as they do to doctors and high achievers. I couldn't get admission in a medical college and felt rejected for many years. I thought that life is a series of troubles and I had no way out. I was working like a donkey in my day job. I was extremely aggressive, frustrated, depressed and overly reactive because I was facing troubles at home as well as at my workplace.

People were cheating on me continuously whether they were my students, friends or colleagues. I just used to curse myself and ask why I was not clever enough. Why do they just take advantage of me and prove me a bad person? Was everyone innocent except me?

Then, my life turned around and my positive thoughts, intentions and prayers were answered.

A wave of life took me out of that low phase of being a "victim." I came to the United Kingdom for higher studies and connected with people who lived at a similar frequency as mine. This was a big relief for my soul. I got much solitude and personal time, which my soul longed for years. I took a break from running after so called goals and targets to become successful and adaptable to the society's rules and values. I set my soul free to find out the how's, why's and what's of my true purpose, growth and development.

"Cease trying to work everything out with your minds. It will get you nowhere. Live by intuition and inspiration and let your whole life be Revelation."
~Eileen Caddy

The ups and downs in our lives are like the crests and troughs of a wave. They teach us vital lessons and clearing negative blocks/beliefs so we can learn and move to the other phases of life. When you reach a peak, you understand the materialistic and extroverted view of life and feel successful.

"Trust my intuition to deliver powerful visions of my inspired future, and I empower my intent to transform those visions into reality."
~Jonathan Huie

The difficult part is the "trough" where everything seems difficult and boring. A person needs space to move on. The journey from trough to crest is exciting and fulfilling when people release old thought forms, people and memories. **Resistance** in any phase can prolong/disturb the process and can result in pain and traumas. Fixation must be resolved in every phase of life. Don't stick to limiting/negative ideas, people, places and circumstances. If you are obsessed with an old beloved who has left you, the reason can be your insecurity or fears. Trust that the higher self will connect you with someone of frequency at the right time.

"Try to realize it's all within yourself no one else can make you change, and to see you're only very small and life flows on within you and without you."
~ George Harrison

Remember, you are a part of these waves. These waves bring new frequencies and take away old ones. We all have the ability to feel the vibration of events before time however we may not be able to interpret the event. We may feel irritated or agitated and may react to it even though it's not related to us. For example: I felt irritated when there was a terrorist attack just two miles away from my house. I felt discomfort before the event.

Sometimes, you just need to stop and understand the information. Just let it pass, and you will understand once it has happened.

Create a Balanced Life

There must be a balanced development in all the areas of life. Equal focus is required for the development of the body, mind and emotions. When a high energy wave flows through a soul, it affects all aspects mentioned above (spiritual to mental to emotional and physical realm) and then flows out of you. If all aspects of awareness are developed evenly, the wave will pass through evenly. Your understanding about yourself and happenings in life will improve. When you don't understand the emotional reality and prefer logic, then awareness has to adjust at a lower level and affects the physical reality i.e. you may experience difficulties in the motivation of completing tasks and feel agitation.

"The best and safest thing is to keep a balance in your life, acknowledge the great powers around us and in us. If you can do that, and live that way, you are really a wise man."
~Euripides

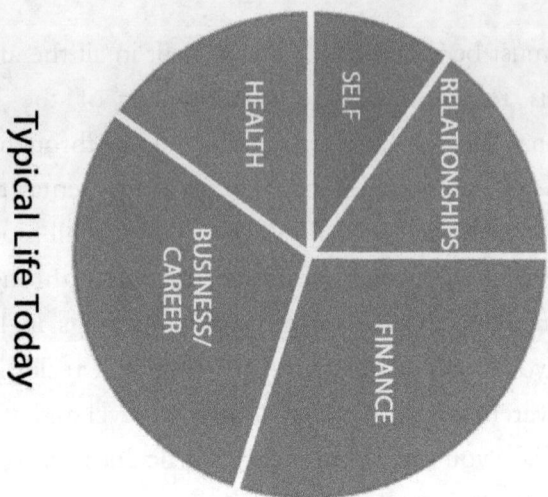

Typical Life Today

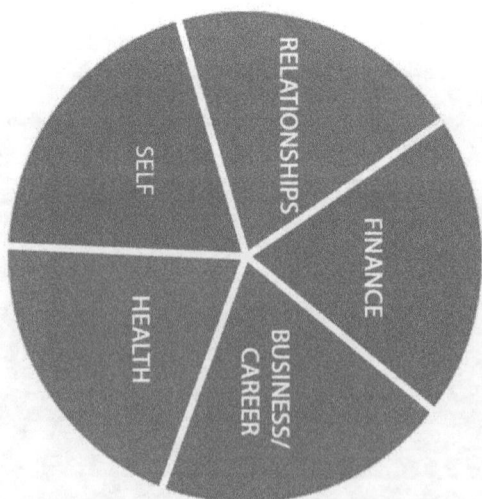

Balanced/Fulfilled Life

© Maddy Malhotra

154

Raise Your Personal Vibrations

"I think in metaphysical terms, I would call that increasing the speed of the vibration of life."
~Neale Donald Walsch

Negative vibrations grab you when you don't feel the presence of the higher self. Your life is surrounded by fears, lies and bad experiences. Personal vibration can be sensed and identified whenever you are angry, fearful or negative. It's like the darkness that surrounds you whenever you are away from love and positive emotions. You will develop more negative feelings and habits.

Take deep breaths to raise your frequency. Smile and recall good things from your life that make you joyful. Don't just use willpower to raise your personal vibrations because that would result in stress and frustration. Clear mental and emotional clutter, first, which actually lowers your vibration.

Deep Breathing Exercises

Breathing helps in bringing our vibrations back to positivity, raise them and provide deep relaxation. It's is a continuous activity performed by our body. It controls the functioning as well as the mental and emotional responses of the body. We breathe in and out about 21,600 times a day. According to yoga experts, breathing is the most important link between the mind and body, as it helps in controlling the mind.

"When the breath wanders the mind also is unsteady. But when the breath is calmed the mind too will be still, and the yogi achieves long life. Therefore, one should learn to control the breath."
~Svatmarama, Hatha Yoga Pradipika

Deep breathing is used as a relaxation technique. I do the following exercises like many other healthy people. Please consult your GP or a health worker before doing these exercises if you have any emotional, psychological and physical problems.

"Focusing on the act of breathing clears the mind of all daily distractions and clears our energy enabling us to better connect with the Spirit within."
~Anon

Here are a few simple breathing techniques for you to try:

1. Sit or lie down comfortably. Gently close your eyes and relax your mind and body. Make sure the place is clean and peaceful. Concentrate on the incoming and outgoing breaths. Try not to change the natural rhythm of your breathing; just be conscious of each breath.

2. Relax your body, keep your eyes closed and concentrate on your breathing. Count numbers with each breath while inhaling and exhaling. Inhale a deep breath and count it as one. As you exhale, count it as two. Similarly, when you inhale and exhale the next breath, count it as three and four respectively. Repeat this procedure for 3-5 minutes.

3. Sit in a comfortable position. Your spine should be straight throughout this exercise. Breathe in slowly and count up to four. Hold your breath for a count of four. Then, breathe out counting up to four again. Repeat this procedure for a few minutes and then increase the count.

Basic Yoga Breathing Technique

Yogic breathing, or **pranayama**, is the science of breath control. Yoga breathing increases the concentration and fights away stress. It also results in serenity and peace of mind. **Kapalbhati** is an ancient and effective yoga breathing exercise that helps to cleanse the mind and reduce weight too. During this exercise, the breathing should be short, rapid and strong. It is practiced using a abdominal or diaphragmatic breathing technique. It helps in curing sinus problems, heavy or foggy head or any kind of blockage in the chest.

"For breath is life, and if you breathe well you will live long on earth."
~Sanskrit/Indian Proverb

These are the steps that you would need to follow:

1. Sit comfortably with your back straight.

2. Relax your body and breathe normally (from diaphragm).

3. Now, exhale powerfully and then inhale deeply. Fill your lungs with air. Inhale and exhale through nose.

4. Assist your exhalation by contracting your stomach muscles, and when you inhale, let your stomach relax/stretch.

5. Inhale and exhale with the help of your stomach muscles.

6. Try doing it fast and repeat the whole procedure twenty times.

Moreover, deep breathing, especially kapalbhati, helps in reducing weight and curing many diseases.

Watch a demo at: www.BeHappyandPeaceful.com/yoga

Releasing Blocks

You are surrounded by a few layers of information/truth through which you experience in your reality. The closest reality contains physical information. The layers containing information about emotions, spirit and thought patterns are the next.

> *"We must let go of the life we have planned, so as to accept the one that is waiting for us."*
> *~Joseph Campbell*

Your soul provides you with information and wisdom about yourself and life. Most of us block that information by accumulating emotional clutters hence only little bit of light can pass through it. Shadows caused by traumas, bad memories and scars of pain cause negative energy. Negative energy stops light and positivity to enter in our lives. If someone has been betrayed, multiple times, in his/her life then the pain of those relations stays in his/her body's energy. It can cause illnesses and pains in the physical body.

Releasing negative/stuck emotions can resolve the black spots, and you can receive the white light i.e. wisdom, intuition and divine love. When the blocks are removed, you can cope with the high vibrations of the earth. You feel more love and wisdom around you and you become a part of it. Your vibration increases automatically. The most unhealthy soul blocks are stubbornness, blame, violence, hate and procrastination.

When you pull your energy out of a belief or fixed idea, the shadow moves away and the soul dominates your life. For example if you thought about your ex-partner frequently during the last few years, stop thinking about that person now. You may experience difficulties while pulling out your energy from that relation but once done you will experience freedom and peace.

"People can be more forgiving than you can imagine. But you have to forgive yourself. Let go of what's bitter and move on."
~Bill Cosby

Negative beliefs come from parents, relatives, friends and society. Move out of these negative ideas because this is someone else's voice running in your head.

"It's not the events of our lives that shape us, but our beliefs as to what those events mean."
~Anthony Robbins

Be in the Vicinity of Water

Taking bath, washing hands, and any type of contact with water can lift our vibration .Water has high vibrational characteristic and its vicinity raises vibration. Whenever you feel low and stuck in a negative loop, immersing your hands or body in water can be the best solution to raise your vibration immediately.

Change Your Focus to the Positive

"If I create from the heart, nearly everything works; if from the head, almost nothing."
~Marc Chagall

You must follow the plan given by the higher self, not ego. Human minds seek knowledge and wish to materialize the desires, of the ego, in a short span of time. You need to stop using your logic and stop giving attention to what your soul doesn't like. Turn your thoughts toward soul's qualities like joy, happiness, gratitude, love etc.

"To know what you prefer, instead of humbly saying Amen to what the world tells you, you ought to prefer, is to have kept your soul alive."
~Robert Louis Stevenson

Steps for the Development of Intuition

"Intuition is really a sudden immersion of the soul into the universal current of life."
~Paulo Coelho

The three main steps required in the development of intuition are:

1. Allow ideas to emerge simultaneously from your inner self. Provide them a way to access your conscious mind, which can later change them into actions and results.

2. Use your imagination and stay in the present. The formula for the end result is always hidden in the flow of the present moment. Love and appreciate this moment because it's the way to the fulfillment of your dreams.

3. Cooperate with the universe, go with the flow and avoid feelings of loneliness. Don't use your logical mind in this step.

Explore Yourself:

1.List the new ideas and projects in your mind.

2.One by one visualize yourself acting on each of them.

3.Now rate the intensity of your feelings associated with these ideas on the scale of 1 to 10.

4.Now seek guidance from your inner wisdom and visualize these ideas again one by one.

5.Identify those ideas which were blocked, by your intuition, the most.

6.Delete those ideas from your list.

Your Notes:

162

Imagination

Preview of Life's Coming Attractions

"Imagination is more important than knowledge"
~Albert Einstein

Human beings have been gifted with **Imagination** by which they can build beautiful pictures in their minds. Everything is possible in our imagination. This faculty becomes weak through **inaction.** Dreams are the source of communication with the subconscious and super conscious minds to get awareness about life while imagination bridges the gap between conscious and super conscious mind.

Man plans his life in his mind, which is the receiving and broadcasting point for the vibrations. The only drawback is the under development and improper use of imagination. **Creative** imagination has been used to connect and communicate with divinity and it works automatically. Inspirations are received this way. This is a process of delivery of ideas from the divinity to man. Subconscious mind communicates with us via imagination.

Learning when you consciously entertain an idea, become emotionally involved in the idea, and step up in the idea is essential. You can't even buy a dress unless you can imagine how you would look in it. You can enhance Self-expression and creativity by using your imagination. Imagination serves as a catalyst in enhancing intuition and using the law of attraction in your favor.

You can be intuitive if you live in a pleasant environment. The best part of imagination is its unlimited nature. You can do, have, or be anything you want!

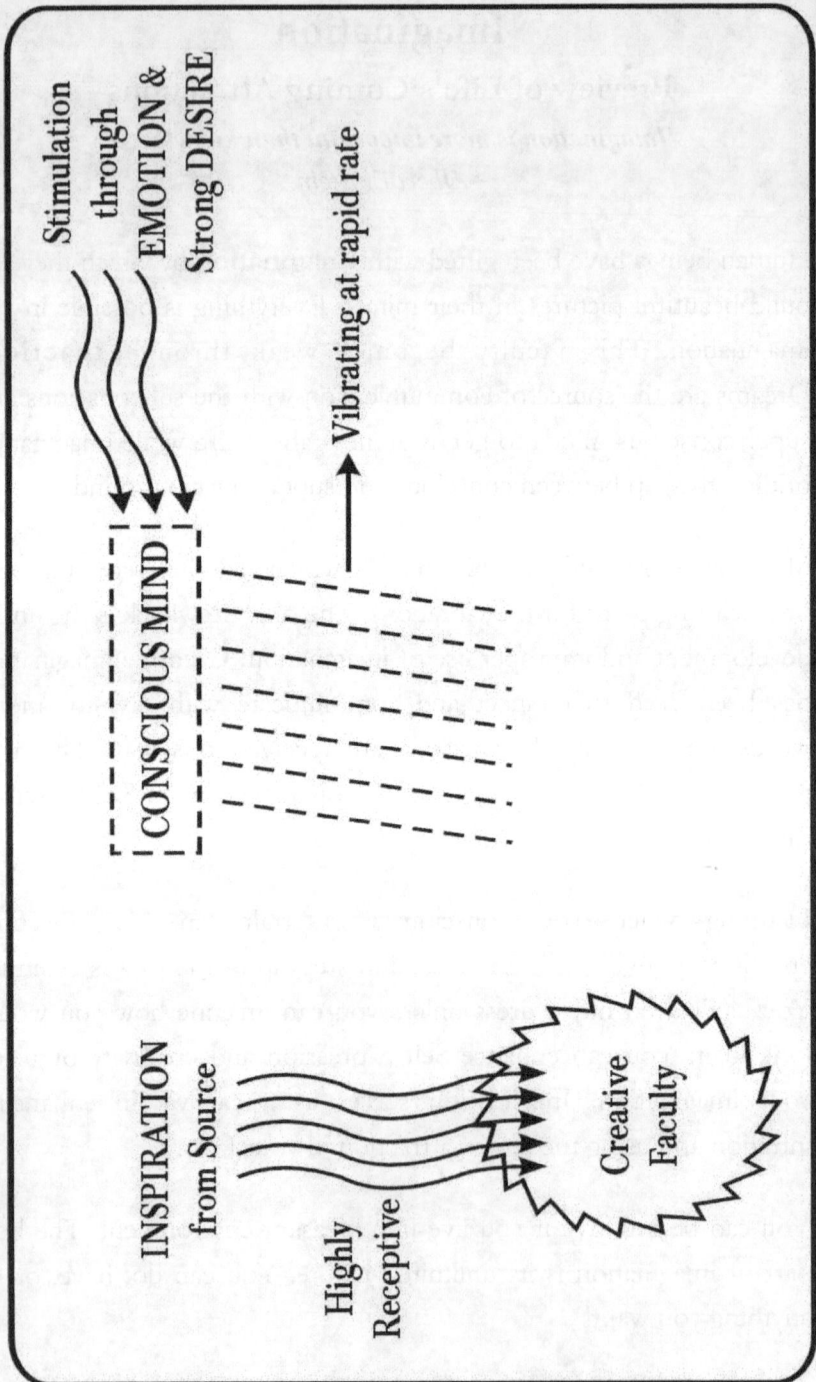

Stimulation through EMOTION & Strong DESIRE

Vibrating at rapid rate

CONSCIOUS MIND

INSPIRATION from Source

Highly Receptive

Creative Faculty

Explore Yourself

Write five desires of yours while imagining you have all the resources to achieve them.

Explore Yourself

1. List any three things/experiences which were part of your imagination and were materialized. Did you initially believe you would get the results?

2. What can you do to activate your creativity in the next few days?

Explore Yourself:

1. Ask a colleague, friend or family member to show you a picture of someone whom you don't know.

Then use your intuition to write the following about the person in the picture:

i. His/her interests

ii. Major problems these days

iii. Appearance

iv. Your feelings about that person? Whether you feel good or bad?

Find out Your Own Symbols

Symbols are a part of imagination and they give important information to us. They can give us hard feelings or provide ways to connect with the super conscious.

Explore Yourself:

1. You can ask your body and the higher self to facilitate the development of your intuition process.

2. Close your eyes and

3.Write which image appears in your mind?

4.Look around and see other images.

You are your own interpreter. All answers you need are inside you. Imagine yourself as the image/symbol you found (it can be a tree, car, star or anything). Be it for a few minutes. You and the symbol will exchange knowledge with each other. If your symbol is a rabbit, enter into it in your imagination. Stay calm and communicate with it. You will get some guideline for yourself.

 This connection helps you to download knowledge which moves you far away from the narrow thinking of the logical mind.

Explore Yourself:

Imagine you are on a long walk and, for example, you find

1. An arrow
2. A crown
3. An apple
4. Keys

Then one by one enter in to each symbol and communicate with it. Exchange your thoughts, knowledge and feelings. It's the best technique to work with your symbols.

Explore Yourself:

Imagine your best friend as a symbol.

Name of your Best Friend:

Flavor (if he/she is edible):

Texture:

Color:

Geometric Shape:

Speed:

Rhythm:

The correlation between symbols and actual sensation is very strong.

Your Notes:

True Frequency
Frequency of love/God/Soul

"God is a frequency. Stay tuned."
~Alan Cohen

We must not expect all new learning to be easily adopted and accepted by our subconscious & conscious minds. People repeat negative actions many times because they are habitual of those patterns. We must be careful about creating beliefs around the 'labels' which others gives us.

We feel weak when mystics, astrologers, numerologists or psychics predict something negative/limiting about us. An astrologer and a psychic, at two different occasions, predicted that I will not be able to travel/live abroad unless I get married. At that time I realized that if I believe them and add worry and anxiety to my life then I will not achieve my desired results. Initially I kept my mind silent and made no future plan because my planning could have ended up in a mediocre outcome. I decided to be joyful and positive. This created space in my life and freedom for my soul.

I got admission in a very good British university for higher studies and that too without any obstacles. I allowed the universe to work for me without using my **ego-based will power**.

A big task in your life is to find out your "True Frequency".

Whenever you feel hopeless, move back to your actual state which is love, hope, joy and happiness i.e. your true frequency. When you get rid of the old habits which no longer serve you then new healthy habits and beliefs are formed. Don't try to control your life by using **ego-based will power**.

"Don't live down to expectations. Go out there and do something remarkable."
~Wendy Wasserstein

Steps to Attain Your True Frequency

"A person who is motivated by anger, selfishness, distrust, and jealousy always has a choice to evolve and achieve a new level where Love, compassion, forgiveness and truth replace these lower drives. In other words, Spirit responds to your vision of it, and the higher your vision, the more you will evolve."
~Deepak Chopra

1. Sit in a quiet place and calm yourself.
2. Try to stop the negative self-talk and pessimistic thoughts.
3. Change your victim mentality to a blessed one. Feel that God gives special attention to you and blesses you every moment.
4. Let the energy flow through your body. Take a deep breath and empty your mind. Feel the energy around you. That's your true frequency.
5. Think about the qualities of your true self: innocence, playfulness, love, cheerfulness and joy. Tap in to your true frequency & vibration with which you came in to this world.
6. Let this vibration spread around yourself.
7. Now visualize that this new frequency is reprogramming your cells. Enjoy this experience to the fullest. All new emotions will be positive and healthy if they come out of this new space. These emotions can be related to anything in your life whether it's the issues, relationships or goals.

Once you are at your true frequency you don't need to use your own force. Allow the wave of energy to take you wherever it goes. Don't listen to your ego and subconscious mind. Your soul will provide you whatever you need.

"It took me a long time not to judge myself through someone else's eyes." ~Sally Field

Decide to Live at Your True Frequency

"Happiness is not something readymade. It comes from your own actions."
~Dalai Lama

There is one stage in everyone's life where an individual makes a decision to feel happy. You decide that you must not wait for the situations and people to take away your problems. At this stage you feel the importance of your life and realize that every moment can be enjoyable. Ask yourself tough questions like "Am I a big hindrance for my growth?" or "Am I creating pain in my body to get other people's attention?"

Take power back from people, events, and memories that move you away from your true frequency. Whenever you are away from your true frequency you will know it. The habit of living in your true frequency will not let you stay in the phase of negativity. Be kind to yourself and choose true frequency again and again. Gradually your circumstances and relationships will be a match of your true vibrations.

Exploring the Secrets of Your Subconscious Mind

"All your new experiences, positive or negative are meant to further your progress and understanding."
~Penney Peirce

Once you have experienced living in your super conscious state, you will crave for it all the time. Practicing intuition, initially, may cause irritation, confusion or aggression. This new way isn't something ordinary. This is your way to **enlightenment**.

You can call it a pure white light which can remove all the impurities from your body. All of these blocks are required to show up in order to be released. There are many experiences in our lives which we call as dark spots. Unfortunately, we make decisions based on the darkness which in reality, comes only for our lessons. We must re-live them and get freedom from the bad shadows in our lives. To make the best choices in life, you should always use your intuition. Sometimes our current losses and pains are actually sources for releasing grief, anxieties and pressures. If you continuously focus on one problem, e.g. career dissatisfaction, then you may get ill and during that period of illness, you will lose focus.

Many parents are very possessive for their children, especially in South Asia. Children have to follow the dreams which are usually created by society, religion and family. They don't think about the aptitude of their child or their children's purpose in life. If someone's purpose is to be an artist then how can he/she become an accountant? The outcome of this can be health problems or other negative experiences/emotions which may be experienced immediately after wrong decisions are made or in the long run.

"If you bring forth what is within you, what you bring forth will save you. If you do not bring forth what is within you, what you do not bring forth will destroy you."
~Gospel of Thomas

Every Child has a Purpose

Every child is naturally intuitive but that ability is blocked by the unhealthy interactions with the parents. Every child can't be exactly like his/her parents. When parents enforce their will on their children it results in a low self-esteem and if they take decisions against their parents and move forward, they face rejection from their parents. That hits their self-esteem.

Every child has his own destiny/purpose in life. When real purpose calls a person's soul, then there is no other way for the soul other than to follow its purpose.

The Universe always gives us a wakeup call to come out of the rat race of earning money, competition, and show off etc. The purpose of the nudges from the Universe is to connect people with their super conscious for some time. Once this connection has been experienced, one can only strive for more. This turning point can be betrayal in love or relationships, loss in business, accident or death of a loved one. At this stage people like to read books on spiritualism or psychology, start meditating, seek help for the satisfaction of this new kind of hunger. This change including praying, meditation, reading books or learning from a spiritual leader allows the super conscious to be a part of our conscious mind. Gradually intuition becomes a part of our daily life.

We must use our power of choice for identifying the real self and we can choose to feel unlucky or try to learn while life unfolds itself.

When we go against our soul, the probability of getting stuck in the process is high. Most people follow thought patterns ingrained in their subconscious minds. They act according to that conditioning but actually they are on the path of troubles and obstacles. When we are stuck, we should stop ourselves and let the Higher Self guide us to resolution.

It is OK to not do or know something. Pull your thoughts out of the past and the future and focus in the present.

"By suspending your thoughts you will enjoy the small things in your life by feeling burning insights and motivations. This will result in a peak of creativity. Try to understand and realize the hidden messages in your life events and intuitions."

~Anon

Explore Yourself :

1. Recall those experiences which worked as a breakthrough in your life?
2. Write down the events which were shocking or overwhelming for you.
3. Did you pray or ask for help?
4. What answers did you receive at that time?
5. What conclusions did you derive at that time?
6. Did those experiences increase closeness between you and God/Inner Self?

When you decide to move ahead these inner blockages become your greatest enemies. You experience a lot of problems and difficulties. You have two options, either to be full of love or full of fear. Subconscious view can hinder intuition and has the capacity to build new blocks. The real meaning of negative events/experiences can be understood by viewing and understanding them from the super conscious view.

Your Notes:

Exercise: Your Reactions

1. Write the details of five situations from your life which created challenges for you.
2. What were your reactions and what did you say to yourself?
3. For example, what happened when someone lied to you? Or you lost your keys when you needed them the most?
4. Did you react from your subconscious mind or super conscious mind?
5. If you did from subconscious mind, rewind all those situations in your mind and respond according to the super conscious mind.

Your Notes:

Your Notes:

Steps for Transformation to Acquire Positive Insights

1. Keep Track of Your Thoughts & Stop Blaming:

Sometimes people feel responsible for the behaviors of other people and circumstances. "I am not good enough", "I can't be rich" and "Life is rubbish". Stop yourself immediately when these thoughts emerge in your head. Tell yourself that it is like a whirlpool and I don't want to be caught in it again.

2. Let Things Happen :

Even if you don't like things, let them be/happen in the way they are. Sometimes we don't find a reason for how & why something happened? You must realize that everything in this universe is happening perfectly in its own way.

3. Be Responsible for Your Reaction :

You must take of control your emotions rather than letting people or circumstances control your behavior. If your spouse or friend didn't keep his/her promise then there is no need to induce negative emotions because there can be a good reason, behind it, which you aren't aware of. Maybe they had some difficulty or change in priority.

4. Believe in Your Reality:

Focus on the now and on your body. Tell yourself that you are a part of the Divine. Everyone needs to grow and understand his/her real self and power. Always repeat in your mind that you are bigger than your problems and realize your true ability/power.

5. Understand Messages from Your Body:

If you experience different kinds of negative emotions like anger, jealousy and frustration then don't run away from them. Feel those emotions which are created as a by-product. People usually refuse to acknowledge these emotions. Your body has an ability to bring itself to the natural state. When it detects anything different than its natural state then you feel uncomfortable (unhealthy emotions) but let it happen. Suppression is not a solution. Listen to your body's voice because it talks to you.

6. Allow Natural Sensations:
Allow natural sensations of your body to flow. It can be a sensation in your belly or change in the blood pressure levels. Remove blocks which create hindrances in the flow. Maybe you need to identify the problem within a specific part of your body or you need to recall some negative events and then release the negative emotions from it.

7. Use Internal Wisdom:
Try to understand all the details of what's happening to you using your internal wisdom. Explore the hidden reasons behind it. You can't change or control other people's behavior and circumstances.

8. Give Time to Your Body:
Gradually your body will become habitual and adjust to the new pattern you have adopted.

Follow the Plan of your Soul

Manifestation process goes through the following steps, whether you want material, people or any experience. When you want anything an experience, people or material, it appears in your imagination, its vibration slows down. The idea is not centuries away from you, as it enters into your personal vibration and it passes through all levels of the brain. It becomes real to your own body and gradually, it becomes real.

An idea becomes reality when you need it on your path to growth. Any good thing which becomes your reality is a function of love and optimism.

We all have various lessons to learn and things to achieve. People come in and leave our lives for this purpose. Your circumstances show up in your life according to the plan of your soul. It knows when you need pain, lessons, or surprises. Your world shapes itself according to your vibrations. Optimism and negativity, dark and light, love and fear, all are a part of life hence your soul goes through your blocks, fixed beliefs, and fears alongside positive things.

Whatever you want to see in reality you must be able to feel it. If you want to have a new house, visualize it in detail. What colors do you see on the walls? Can you see the furniture, garden, and kitchen? How does it impact your life emotionally? Who else is with you?

Explore Yourself :

1. Ask a friend or a family member to participate in this exercise
2. Sit face to face and close your eyes.
3. In the space between the two of you, visualize something, which both of you want, moving towards both of you.
4. If its money then both of you must describe the smell, size, shape, feeling, amount and every little detail to each other.
5. Imagine sending light to that money and then let it go.

Wait for the response from the universe. You do not know when and how it will happen, but you need to believe that **it will** happen!

Your Notes:

Your Body is the Best Guide

Body is a great companion, which gives us a guideline about our choices. It guides us about the right actions at the right time. It tells us whether it's a **matter of survival** or **higher guidance** from our soul and the collective unconscious. It can communicate in the form of "yes" or "no" which may be expressed through contraction, expansion, blush, and tears of happiness.

If something isn't good for you and the answer from the body is "No "then your body's immediate response can be contraction. People experience energy drops or then behave in a cold way with other people. Most people are aware about the **No** signals as compared to the **Yes** ones.

If we learn to understand these signals then we can find a way to seek wisdom about the self and life.

Ask your body to give you a response, whenever you feel difficulty in making decisions.
Ask your body -What would you like for the next meal?
Would you like vegetables, meat, or something in liquid form?
This strategy can be used in making life decisions!
Your body can guide you about the kind of day job you must do?

Imagine what kind of sensations you experience after imagining every option you have. Would you like to sit in front of a computer for 10 hours every day? Your body will answer you instantly. Act on the desires of your body and it will be your best guide.

Take a deep breath and ask a question from your body, "What should I do in this moment?

Whenever your body has a message for you it talks to you, sometimes you feel irritated or disturbed. You don't listen to it, it whispers again and again. Finally there is a red light for you; it may be in the form of disease. You will start getting emotional signals like we all experience unknown sadness sometimes this may be because you have an underlying feeling that no one likes you.

If you do not release these negative emotions, they will gather more energy and turn in to an uncontrollable beast. When you suppress the stored energy, it emerges in the form of physical symptoms like headaches, heart burn, or indigestion. Your negligence towards your emotions can increase your physical pain. Your chronic abdominal pain has the potential to turn in to a cancer and chest pain can result in heart attack. When you are seriously ill but you don't listen to your body then something tragic can happen in your life like an accident, a divorce or a robbery, which causes you to stop and pay attention to your body.

Lisa, one of my clients, was under stress because of her full time job, kids, and her husband's bad behavior. These stressors created distress in her life. She suffered from back pain, stomach issues, and headaches. But she continued with pain killers without giving attention to her core issues. After six months, she had a mild chest pain, which was alarming for her. Doctors told her she was vulnerable to heart attack. She suffered a heart attack after a few weeks! Her body was warning her continuously, to slow down and resolve the issues which were creating extra pressure on her body. Sometimes the first step towards a solution is to listen to the signals from your own body.

If you keep blaming your luck then the energy of your body drops and you lose your ability to cope with the world. Consequently, there are higher chances of becoming insane, committing suicide or developing phobias or even paralysis. The last stage is death because the expression of the soul is blocked. It has no way to break through the conscious mind.

Explore Yourself :

1. Keep a track of your state of mind. If it's distracted, it needs your attention. You may be feeling angry, irritated, or burdened.
2. Sit in a quiet place, close your eyes, and talk to your body. You will get all the negative labels your conscious mind has given to that state of your body. Remove all those labels. Just feel the sensations because they guide you for betterment.
3. Let the energy flow in your body, you have to just observe where it flows. If in the diaphragm, take a few deep breaths. If in the legs and/or arms, then do some exercise. Observe your throat, whether you feel energy there or not? If yes, then what do you want to say and to whom?
4. When energy reaches your brain, pay attention to the sensory information, thoughts, feeling, and emotions. What did you find/learn?

Explore Yourself :

1. What do you understand about your true nature?
2. What do you appreciate about your body most?
3. What's the most powerful attribute in your personality?
4. Which is the most beautiful part of your body?

Write down the response of your body while doing this exercise.

Your Notes:

SECTION NO: 3

When you want to attract something into your life, make sure your actions don't contradict your desires. Think about what you have asked for, and make sure that your actions are mirroring what you expect to receive, and that they're not contradicting what you've asked for. Act as if you are receiving it. Do exactly what you would do if you were receiving it today, and take actions in your life to reflect that powerful expectation. Make room to receive your desires, and as you do, you are sending out that powerful signal of expectation.

~Rhonda Byrne

The Law of Attraction

"You will attract everything that you require. If its money you need you will attract it. If its people you need you'll attract it. You've got to pay attention to what you're attracted to, because as you hold images of what you want, you're going to be attracted to things and they're going to be attracted to you. But it literally moves into physical reality with and through you. And it does that by law."
~Bob Proctor

The Law of Attraction is one of those laws that control the conversion of the creative energy in to physical reality. Energy flows where attention goes. Your thoughts are like magnets and you attract people, circumstances and things which are harmonious with your dominant thoughts. You can attract at spiritual, mental and physical level. Your circumstances are a reflection of what goes inside you. You don't attract what you want, you attract what you are. If you are suffering in life then change your thoughts. You will see a change in your circumstances and experiences if you successfully change your dominant thoughts and beliefs to positive ones. If you use passion with your dreams and desires, manifestation will be quicker. In other words if your affirmations, visualization (both are explained in this section later) etc. will be charged with emotions then you will get quicker results.

Law of attraction always works in the present moment. It doesn't matter what kind of vibrations you offered few minutes ago. You can change your vibrations any time. The only thing that matters in the present moment is your decision. It will give you more of the same of what you are sending right now.

You should train yourself to reach the source of vibrations within you. You are a free-will being and you have the ability to focus on what you want. Either you can worry or you can look for the reasons to feel good. What you practice becomes dominant in your vibration.

Your thought attracts other thoughts of equivalent frequency. This leads to the creation of chronic thoughts and then chronic beliefs.

Repetitive thoughts >> Chronic thoughts >> Chronic beliefs

↓ Law of attraction

↓ Pattern of vibrations

The Law of attraction responds to your feelings. You are the thinker who projects thoughts and the law manages all of the thoughts that exist. You must pay attention to your thoughts because thoughts become things.

The higher self is the biggest part of you. You should understand the relationship between you who exists externally and you (Spirit) in the physical body. You can achieve whatever you want if you bring these two in alignment. For example

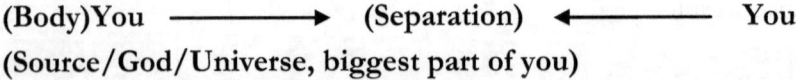

(Body)You ⟶ (Separation) ⟵ You (Source/God/Universe, biggest part of you)

If you want to attract what you want you must be in alignment with the higher self. Vibrations of the higher self are love, peace and joy and by default your desires are at high vibrations. If you align yourself with the vibrations of the higher self only then you will be aligned with what you want to receive.

(Now)You ⟷ You (What you want to be) (Separation)

You ⟷ You = YOU (Aligned) Desires are manifested.

When you are joyous you are a blend of you and you. When you are in an irritated mood the you and you are separated.

The decision is always yours, whether you separate you (What you are now) from you (What you want to be) or not which is the alignment of what you are outside and what your soul is. Remember our soul is a part of higher self. If you dwell on the emotions/feelings like insecurity, competition, jealously or lack of self-love, it indicates that you are at a distance from your true self.

> *"Your life is in your hands. No matter where you are now, no matter what has happened in your life, you can begin to consciously choose your thoughts, and you can change your life. There is no such thing as a hopeless situation. Every single circumstance of your life can change!"*
> ~Rhonda Byrne

Most people think that more money, big house, perfect spouse, thin and perfect body would ensure the betterment of their lives. Moreover they think they can get whatever they want by using the law of attraction. But they aren't aware of other laws of the universe especially the law of karma. If they become selfish and attract something for the satisfaction of their ego, karma will come back in the form of negative events, people, situations etc. Bad karma brings back negative experiences.

Spiritual identity is the core ingredient of life. People try/intend to achieve targets with the wrong use of will power while using the law of attraction in their favor. They want to achieve for satisfying their ego and to show off to the society. Many times, they act out of their insecurity. When people deliberately attract things for selfish reasons then their connection with the higher self is lost.

It doesn't mean that we must wait to become lucky one day.

We must learn a way to create a balance between our material and spiritual needs. People who use their will power to manifest everything believe solely in themselves and only in their own efforts. They forget that the universe has a purpose for everyone. Their approach may be helpful in the short term but after sometime, they are unable to get the same results! If they get their desired results again and again and those results aren't in alignment with the plan of their soul then they face difficulties in what they have manifested. For example if someone has used his/her willpower, or prayed etc. to manifest material wealth, more than the universe had planned for them, without consulting their intuition then that person has to go through challenges/troubles in multiple areas of their lives!

"Faith is not the belief that God will do what you want. It is the belief that God will do what is right."
~Max Lucado

I have seen many people who are desperate to marry a specific person and they are ready to pay any cost for it. Those who were meant to be together will be together and enjoy their lives. Few people manage to marry who they like by using their personal force even if they had to face difficulties. But they forget a reality: The universe wasn't in the favor of that relationship which is why they faced difficulty. They weren't on same frequency/soul mates. In the long run this relation could be painful. So the Universe wants to save us from pains of the future that's why it creates obstacles. We must learn to listen to our intuition which guides us for betterment.

"Many people in Western culture are striving for success. They want the great home, they want their business to work, and they want all these outer things. But what we found in our research is that having these outer things does not necessarily guarantee what we really want, which is happiness. So we go for these outer things thinking they're going to bring us happiness, but it's backward. You need to go for the inner joy, the inner peace, and the inner vision first, and then all of the outer things appear."
~Marci Shimoff

Desire

"Offer a vibration that matches your desire rather than offering a vibration that keeps matching what-is."
~Abraham

Desire is the effort of an **unexpressed possibility** within us that seeks expression through us. It is a way of communication for the spirit, and everybody wants to give birth to some desires. Everybody has something within them which they want to give to the world but few people get to experience their internal desires. You will not be able to make your desires a reality until you don't visualize and take action towards achieving them.

Expectation is an important ingredient for attraction. One of the reasons why we catch cold in the winter is because we see that in adverts and expect it to happen. Our expectations are magnetic and will attract everything of a like nature. Everybody wants to realize his/her dreams, but usually people stop due to crisis, comfort zone or disbelief. People who dream and focus on their goals must be ready to take risks.

The mind has unlimited powers. When there are demands and risks, our mind shows us various options. These options include fears, worries, insecurities, hope, happiness, success etc. Usually people expect what they don't want. The magnetic pull of expectation brings results in their lives according to the selected options.

 Expectation is the most powerful unseen force in our lives; it can either be a blessing or curse. If you are full of worries regarding your exam results, chances of failure increase. Take a piece of paper, make a list of all the subjects and write your desired grade against each.

Enjoy your success daily with the help of imagination and emotions; chances of getting good grades are high if you do this exercise. This doesn't mean that you can achieve good grades without hard work ☺

Determine your dominant state of mind instead of your circumstances. Bad circumstances can be a result of negative thinking. Use expectation as a triggering mechanism to bring good things in your life. **But this doesn't mean that we shouldn't be open for the plan of the higher self (as discussed in the intuition chapter***)***. We may experience failures and disappointments while we use the tools and techniques for manifestation. That could mean that something better has been planned for us which we aren't aware of. Universe always works in our favor whether we realize it or not!

"Desire is the starting point of all achievement, not a hope, not a wish, but a keen pulsating desire which transcends everything."
~Napoleon Hill

Explore Yourself :

Recognize the difference between "What you want" and "what you have been expecting". Search deep within your own feelings and describe what you have been expecting in your life up to this point.

Your Notes:

The Slight Edge : Turning Simple Disciplines into Massive Success & Happiness

"The truth is, what you do matters. What you do today matters. What you do every day matters. Successful people just do the things that seem to make no difference in the act of doing them and they do them over and over and over until the compound effect kicks in."
~Jeff Olson

Sometimes just one step or one idea is required for achieving big, but we don't take appropriate action to make it a reality. The line which separates winning from losing is as defined as slight edge for example someone has a unique idea but he/she didn't implement it while on the other side another person gets the same idea and takes action on it.

Persistence is the characteristic that makes you stand out. So, the next time you step out to do something and **"the going gets tough,"** just remember that the Slight Edge for you could well be your own ability to persevere. Just try one more time with enthusiasm, and you may see your accomplishments go from ordinary to extraordinary!

Explore Yourself:

List six Slight Edge Actions you will implement immediately that will make significant difference in your life.

Your Notes:

202

How to Improve Self-Image?

"The self-image is the key to human personality and human behavior. Change the Self-Image and you change the personality and the behavior."
~Maxwell Maltz

Self-image is a base of our entire personality and it's essential to work on it before deliberate creation. Improving self-image can help you to get what you want. People spend their whole lives, but they don't understand their desires and the benefits of a better self-image. Imagine what you want to become, in your subconscious mind, and repeat it often. Your life will change. The knowledge of image-making can eliminate competition from your life by moving you from a competitive mindset to a creative one. Actually, one competition exists, and that is with your own ignorance. The results which you have in your life are the physical manifestation of the images in your subconscious mind. You have to improve your own image in your subconscious mind.

Cybernetics

Cybernetics was defined in the mid-20th century by Norbert Wieneras "**the scientific study of control and communication in the animal and the machine**." The word "cybernetics" comes from the Greek meaning to "**steer**" or "**navigate**." Biological organisms and some machines have sensors, which determine their deviation from a set target. These sensors help in correcting the behaviour or output of machines because the nervous system or coordinating system gets the feedback from this source.

Psycho cybernetics

(Psycho means mind) and (**Cybernetics is science of control and communication**) in our marvellous mind. Maxwell Maltz (1899 – 1975) was an American cosmetic surgeon and author of Psycho-Cybernetics(1960), which was a system of ideas that he claimed could improve one's self-image. In turn, the person would lead a more successful and fulfilling life.

> *"It's not what you are that holds you back; it's what you think you're not."*
> ~Denis Waitley

For example, one sales person has a self-image that he can earn 3million per year. One year, he earned 5 million and, as a result of that (sensor/self-image) system, sent a message to the subconscious mind about results that are different than the target. Next year, his sales reduced to 3million per year. Then, next year, he couldn't earn money. At that time, the system/self-image picked that information and sent information about the changed results. The salesman started sales again, and at the end of year, he earned 3 million again. This person has an image in his mind that he does sales of 3 million per year. One year, his sales value rose up to 5 million. The system (self-image) identified a change and sent message to bring it back at a particular threshold. That's why that person came back to 3 million per year. Same thing happened when his sales went down.

Explore Yourself:

1.Relax yourself and Do meditation/breathing exercise.

2.Write a description of the person you want to become in detail (present tense) i.e. I am assertive girl and I am living my purpose etc.

3. Read and Visualize that description because our mind obeys our voice most.

4. If possible record and listen to that description of your desired self daily.

One essential requirement of the new you (improved self-image) is to learn optimism. Describe your desired self in positive words and present tense. Keep one thing in your mind: that your new self doesn't know anything about your past. It's the present that really counts. Writing is very important because when you write, new brain cells develop. These brain cells store the image of the new you. You must relax yourself daily, which triggers these new brain cells, and every time you repeat the process, it delivers more energy to these cells. Visualize regularly what you have written.   .

For example you can write that " My name is _____. I am a successful painter and I am highly motivated and dedicated to my work. I am happy with my family. I know how to maintain balance in different areas of life.

You can write according to the changes you want in different areas of life.

The inner power of creativity will express this image into your life. Write this description multiple times, you can add or delete details whenever you want. As people do visualization for the manifestation of their desires, if possible write and read your new self-descriptions daily. Every time after writing, it will become clearer. If possible record an audio of your written description in your own voice because our mind recognizes our own voice most. Listen to it whenever you have time at least once a day.

When you add energy of emotions in desired self-image and make it better regularly, it indicates that you are moving in the vibrations of desired image. It will become your reality with the help of the power inside you. Even you don't believe what you write on the page, and maybe you call it silly. In the beginning "New You" will remain fantasy for you but by doing exercise regularly, it will turn into a theory in your mind .In a short period of time, you won't think it silly any more. That will be your reality, and this past self will not exist anywhere.

Your Notes:

Your Notes:

Steps for the " Manifestation Process"

"Your prayer causes you to focus, and the Law of Attraction *causes everything in the Universe that's in vibrational harmony with your focus to come to you."*
~Abraham

When I studied the law of attraction, I felt as if I got the key to success. A secret which can help me manifest anything with the blink of an eye. I started following the instructions with complete acceptance and passion and waited for the manifestation of my desires anxiously. I even followed the steps which gurus taught: Ask >> believe >> receive. I did positive affirmations day and night. I visualized accomplishing my goals and even maintained a vision book/journal (explained later). I started working on my beliefs, guilt, anger etc. to release my mental blocks. I followed all the instructions given in the book 'The Secret' religiously. There were a few goals/dreams which weren't realized on certain dates as mentioned in books, documentaries and workshop DVDs for the law of attraction. Many of my dreams always remained dreams.

The information I got through "The Secret" and the so called 'law of attraction gurus' was great but sorry to say it was incomplete! Incomplete information is sometimes more dangerous than ignorance. I had many questions in my mind. It was very difficult to get answers. I was so disappointed in myself because I followed the instructions religiously but didn't get the expected results. The result was self-blame and guilt because I thought I was not capable of following instructions and of changing myself. But found out it wasn't just me! Hundreds of thousands of people complained the same.

After a long period of guilt and self-blame I decided to search for important keys which were missing. After much effort of around 3 years I found out a few vital things which weren't mentioned in "The Secret".

That information was incomplete because:
1. It doesn't focus much on taking action.
2. It neglects the role of the higher self and one's purpose in life.
3. There was no such instruction to access/use intuition.
4. The concept of 'cooperation' was missing in the secret. Actually when we make any wish, the whole universe is involved in its manifestation.
Our one decision affects many people's lives which we are unaware. If someone wants to win a lottery, then a large number of people must buy lottery tickets. We don't know whether universe considers that person deserving for the lottery money or the lottery money was part of his soul's purpose or not. People aren't aware of these important factors. They start making selfish wishes but when these kinds of wishes come true, people have to pay huge prices in the form of problems, challenging situations, painful events etc. and then they realize that their demands were not in their favor in the end. In contrast if universe would consider some one deserving of winning lottery then it will manifest without using much personal force in this desire. We must learn to flow with the life.
5. We cannot live happily and peacefully if we have intentions to get what we want by hook or crook. We cannot control our and other people's life for the fulfillment of our desires.

In the past few years people had easy access to the details of the law of attraction and they went crazy to manifest their desires, most of which were related to finance and relationships. A few people who manifested their desires within a fixed time span became the source of turmoil and low self-esteem for the majority who couldn't. I was one of them who couldn't manifest most of the things I dreamt of. I felt depressed and like a failure.

That disappointment increased my curiosity to search answers for my questions. Perhaps at that time my soul was only capable of learning limited knowledge about the law of attraction.

Now I realize that I attracted information when my soul was ready to take it. I believe that timings of the universe are always right. It will provide everything which our soul would need. You just have to trust and let go. It's all about faith. I got whatever my soul needed at the right time. I am constantly working to increase happiness, peace and contentment. I decided to follow the plans of my soul rather than fixed targets based on my deprivations, ego, jealousy or competition. The laws of the universe don't favor those who want to use them in their favor with negative intentions.

After many failures I started reading more books to know the reasons of my failure to manifest (as mentioned in the *introduction*).

I developed intuitive abilities, learned connection with the divine, experienced heart-felt gratitude, learned to do the contribution to the society. I started looking at others as a part of the higher self not judging them by worldly achievements. I realized that forgiveness is an ongoing process and I do it regularly. Above all faith in the divine/universe is the key to happiness and peace which I knew after many pains and difficulty.

Below is a small recipe of action steps which I learned while studying the work of wise people and the ancient wisdom. It worked for me and has helped many of my clients and students.

Thoughts and beliefs are very important for the manifestation process. We must work on our beliefs thoroughly (as mentioned in the previous section). Until you have identified your limiting beliefs for different areas of life, you shouldn't start attracting anything deliberately because they will stop you on your way to betterment. These negative beliefs can hinder intuition process and affect the whole process of deliberate creation. It doesn't mean that just by thinking and believing we will get whatever we want; these are essential contributing factors in the manifestation process.

You can improve the unfulfilled areas of your life. I would like to emphasize here that intuition should always be prioritized in your life. Before following the following steps, setting your goals and visualizing, **consult your intuition and connect to your inner-self**.

These aren't my techniques but I added a few new steps and changed the sequence of these proven steps to get the results which you desire.

1. Identification Step

"Contrast helps you to identify desire. Desire is summoning. It's always flowing through you. You have the opportunity of opening to the harmony of the vibration of your desire or not. As the desires are being summoned through you, and you go with the flow, you thrive, but if you use things to be your excuse for not going with the flow, you are arguing for your limitations. We want to show you how to go with the flow. Which means nothing more than finding vibrational harmony with your own desire and letting the Universal Energy that your desire is summoning to it flow to it through you? It is optimum creative experience."
~Esther Hicks

We are so influenced by our beliefs, emotions and life experiences that we set our goals based on them rather than what we truly want. We usually think about what we don't want in life. The solution for this problem is to find out your desires from all the areas of life(relationships, finance, career, self-healing).

Make a list of desires for every area of life.

When the list is ready then you will be able to find out the specific things which you really don't like. You can't eat food which you don't like similarly you will have to teach your mind to discard the thoughts that aren't good for you. You can utilize your bad experiences for your betterment.

Explore Yourself :

Identification of contrasts will help you in finding out your true desires. You can use this exercise for all the areas of your life.

For example, Make a list of **'What you want'** and **'What you don't want'**. If you want trustworthy and positive friends in your life then make a list of characteristics and habits of a friend whom you don't like. Write the opposite of those negative characteristics (desired positive) in the second Column. Analyze the relationships you had. If you don't like liars, write it down. When your list is complete, delete everything which you don't want and keep a list of 'wants' with you. You should then shift your focus to the "wants". This process will restrict you from dwelling on the negative things.

I do not want	qualities I want
Lie	Truthful
Dominate/are possessive	Supportive
Compete	Cooperative
Are Jealous of my success	Celebrate my achievements

For your job/business:

What I don't want?	What do I want?
Long working hours	less working hours
Bad working environment	friendly & healthy environment
Underpaid	highly paid

Your Notes:

2. Make a list of your desires

After completion of the identification step you may create a list of your desires/dreams/goals. This is a good time to write everything down because your mind will be clear. List your desires against different areas of life (relationships, health, financial success, career, and spirituality, self…)

3. Access your intuition

Be centered, calm down and then follow your inner guidance. By accessing your intuition you save yourself from being shattered and disappointed, in the long run, which people face when they create their goals, do affirmations, change beliefs and visualize without using intuition. Every failure and disappointment usually strengthens negative beliefs in many people's lives. Their condition is worse than the people who aren't aware of the universal laws. They touch peaks of positivity and then slide down. So the best/safe way is to follow your intuition (described in the previous section). Following your intuition doesn't guarantee 100% positive result but at least you will be able to understand what's right for you and what isn't.

If some of your desires aren't fulfilled it means you need to create new goals after seeking inner guidance and try again.

Start attracting what you want by following steps given below.

4. Ask

The law of attraction is a universal law. It has been mentioned in the ancient books and scriptures.

The Bible says *"Ask, and it shall be given you; seek, and ye shall find; knock, and it shall be opened unto you."*

Write down your desires and before that make sure you feel relaxed. It's your choice whether you want to ask for multiple things at a time or just one. You can ask for it by writing it down or by closing your eyes and asking for it in your prayer. You have to broadcast your desires in the universe. Our prayers and desires are vibrations and we are vibrational beings. Your task at this stage is only to "release" your vibration of desire(s) in the universe and trust that you will get replies which are in your highest good. Your desires may be fulfilled or you may receive a guideline to change your desire or you may get signs or omen which will inform you about the time delay of the fulfillment of your desires. You role is to be open for the replies.

5. Believe in Yourself and the Universe

"Your belief determines your action and your action determines your results, but first you have to believe."
~Mark Victor Hansen

At that very moment when you ask for something, the imprint of your desire is created in your mind and the universe starts shaping itself to reply to your desire. Your dominant thoughts and feelings are reflected back to you in your life by the law of attraction. Your beliefs control what you think about everything. Most of the Secret's gurus recommend that you must believe what you desire but most of us find it difficult because we have been programmed the other way round.

"The moment you say, or, the skies will open for you and the non-physical energies begin instantly to orchestrate the manifestation of your desire."
~Esther Hicks

You must have a strong belief in the Universe that it will always support you whether by giving what you want you want or by giving you a new direction. You must tell yourself that you will always get what's in your highest good. When you do that, the law of attraction will powerfully change/move all the circumstances, people or events for you to receive what's best for you. Negative Beliefs always interrupt, when we think positive, and control thoughts and actions unconsciously. When it's difficult to think positive then you must take action to change your beliefs (see the exercises given in the previous section).

"It won't matter if thousands of people believe in you unless you believe in you."
~Maddy Malhotra

6. Faith

Faith is a quality of such high frequency that it transcends the lower laws and makes the impossible possible. Faith allows miracles to happen and it's like an unshakeable rock. It stays solid through rain, hail and mudslides. As such, it confers great power.

The Law of Faith states: If you have total faith in an outcome, it will come about. To the extent that you doubt, you allow the possibility of failure. When you have an absolute, implicit and total trust in the

Divine, you know that whatever is for your greatest good is going to happen. Faith dissolves fears. It means constantly listening to your inner guidance and intuition. Blind faith is different. It implies giving away your trust without foundation for it. The trust is misplaced through lack of discernment.

If you build a house on weak foundations, you will always feel a sense of uncertainty and doubt about its safety. A house with a strong foundation represents security. There may be minor things to amend, but the essence of the house is strong.

"As your faith is strengthened you will find that there is no longer the need to have a sense of control, that things will flow as they will, and that you will flow with them, to your great delight and benefit."
~Emmanuel Teney

Confidence is faith in you. If you have a foundation of high self-esteem and self-worth, you will be a relaxed and easy person to be with. No one can undermine you, for you will trust your own ability and others will intuitively trust you.

When you have faith in a dream, it will succeed (if it's in your highest good). If you don't have faith, ask someone else to hold your vision for you. Their faith will ensure success. I know a proud mother who said about her successful son, "I always knew he would succeed. I had total faith in him." And the son said, "In difficult times, I could hear my mother's voice and knew she believed in me. It gave me the strength to continue."

Faith is not something to grasp, it is a state to grow into."
~Mahatma Gandhi

Faith works like a strong catalyst in your mind. When it's blended with positive thoughts and feelings, vibrations rise. Then, the subconscious mind translates it in to the spiritual equivalents and transmits it to the divinity. As a result, you get what you really want.

The two most powerful emotions are faith and love. When they are mixed together, they can create miracles by speeding up the vibrations and developing direct line of communication between the finite thinking mind of man and the infinite intelligence.

Development of Faith

All experiences have effects on the mind and body. Faith can only be developed by repetition, and the best method to do so is doing affirmations. If you have experience something multiple times, it becomes a belief. So, repeating something can become your faith in the long run. When you practice it regularly, you become perfect.

Affirmations/Self Talk

Affirmations/self-talk is a powerful tool for the development of faith. When something is repeated in the subconscious mind, it becomes reality in the conscious mind of a person. What you really believe, you achieve.

"It's the repetition of affirmations that leads to belief. And once that belief becomes a deep conviction, things begin to happen."
~Claude Bristol

i. Positive Affirmations: A Proven Way to Re-condition The Subconscious Mind

In almost every society, the majority of people complain that they cannot live the life of their dreams. They blame people, circumstances, luck, environment etc. If they just focus on their mental capabilities, they will find that they have been blessed with valuable assets. One factor which contributes in the helplessness of people is *low self-esteem*. The development of low self-esteem/belief is a big obstacle in thinking and acting big.

"The most influential and frequent voice you hear is your inner-voice. It can work in your favor or against you, depending on what you listen to and act upon."
~Maddy Malhotra

To improve your self-esteem you should repeat some positive statements so as the subconscious starts believing in it. You can write those affirmations and/or record them in your own voice and can repeat/listen multiple times a day. This new programming of your mind will change the old hopeless/helpless-self. There are a few encouraging promises ,which one can make to him/herself, which can improve the overall quality of life of an individual. The most essential one is the commitment to follow his/her real purpose in life while being persistent and focusing on life's main aim.

"You become what you think about most of the time."
~Brian Tracy

Remember that your dominating thoughts will materialize themselves in the external world. Repeat your affirmations, at least, twice every day for thirty minutes in total and keep a clear picture of your desires in your mind while repeating those thoughts. Commit to yourself that you will continue your efforts until you achieve your goals.

Your conscious mind understands and obeys your voice more than any other. Every law of attraction teacher suggests using positive words and statements. They ask people to repeat their desire in the present tense using positive statements (for example, "I love and accept myself"). At this point, your mind knows what is true and what isn't. This creates a conflict because when your subconscious mind believes that you hate yourself, how can it suddenly accept your affirmations?

When you repeat something that's not true for your present condition and you don't believe it, you emit a negative vibration. Doubt is the usual outcome of this repetition. Law of attraction responds to your inner feelings, not words! Work on your beliefs and feelings; don't tell a lie to yourself. If you say "I have an ideal relationship with my family" without believing and feeling it then your mind will reject it immediately.

If you say, "I am in the process of creating perfect relationships," that sounds believable. Now, your mind knows that you are speaking the truth (unless you aren't making an effort).

"Any idea, plan, or purpose may be placed in the mind through repetition of thought."
~Napoleon Hill

ii. Steps for Creating Affirmations:
Write your affirmations in your journal.

Step 1: Opening Line Statement:
I am in the process of attracting a likeminded partner.

Step 2: Explanation of Desires:

Make sure you select the words which express your deepest feelings, for example:

I am excited _____

(Example: I am excited for my ideal weight because I am on the way of achieving it)

I love to know _____

(Example: I love to know that I am on the way of liking and approving myself)

I like seeing myself _____

(Example: I like seeing myself as a loving husband/wife)

Step 3: Closing Statement:

The law of attraction is working on (my desire) and rearranging itself to realize (my desire).

iii. Recap for Writing Affirmations:

1. Pick a few things from your desire list for an area of life, which you created while using contrasts.

For example relationships (ideal partner)

Don't Want	Desire
Dominant and possessive	Open minded and friendly
Introvert	Extrovert
Not affectionate	affectionate and loving
Addiction/bad habits	Makes healthy choices/habits

2. Now, write your opening statement.

I am in the process of attracting all I need to do, know or upgrade to attract my perfect partner.

3. Explanation of your desire.

- I enjoy how it feels knowing that my ideal partner is a balanced person.
- I love how it feels that my ideal partner is sensitive, friendly and optimistic.
- I am happy to know that my partner has healthy habits.
- I am excited about the thought of enjoying travelling and seeing the whole world with him/her.

4. Closing statement:

The law of attraction is working on connecting my desired partner with me and rearranging itself to making it real.

7. Use the Power of Focus to Manifest Your Desire

"Nothing can add more power to your life than concentrating all your energies on a limited set of targets."
~NidoQubein

When you need more heat in your room, you just increase the thermostat of your heater. In the same sense, if you want to achieve something in your life, you must increase **attention** towards it. Law of attraction always responds to your current vibration. You need to add your dreams/goals/targets in your present vibration by focusing, positively, on them.

Vibrational Circle:

Imagine that you have a circle of energy which surrounds you. It's your magnetic power through which you can attract anything you want. It's like a **barter system** but in this trade you will get the exact items as you offer. You get what you send out. You get the same kind of experiences, people, things and circumstances that you have in your vibration circle. Positive will attract positive, while negative will result in bad relationships, circumstances and experiences. But sometimes negative experiences are meant to teach you important lessons in life.

Make Your Vibrational Circle Positive*:*
1. Talk about what you desire.
2. Notice if something positive happens to you unexpectedly (e.g. if you receive care from someone that you never expected and wasn't in your wish list).
3.Change your focus and visualize all the good that has happened to you when you:
(i)   Complain about something
(ii) When you have negative memories in your mind
(iii) When you are jealous of something
(iv) When you pray for more
(v)   When someone is rude to you

In all above given conditions, whatever you are doing is included in your vibration circle. It will attract positive or negative depending on whatever you have in your store.

"We can't solve the problem by focusing on and worrying about the problem itself."
~Maddy Malhotra

8. Visualization

"I visualize things in my mind before I have to do them. It's like having a mental workshop."
~Jack Youngblood

Visualization is an essential ingredient for the manifestation process. It serves as a **catalyst** to convert your dreams into reality. Your subconscious mind doesn't know the difference between the reality and the experience of visualization. You can experience anything as real by using this tool. It can activate physiological responses to the situations, and this information is stored in your subconscious mind as a fact.

Our bodies are conditioned according to the repetitive thoughts in our mind, which then create beliefs and emit vibrations according to this programming. The universe responds to the vibrations we emit. Positive visualization can lead to the quick response from the universe in our favor.

Visualize for the Manifestation of Your Dreams
(Do not do this if you suffer with fear of flying/height!)
Sit comfortably, take a deep breath and relax. Imagine that you are standing on a very high mountain. There is nothing between you and the vertical drop. Notice that the weather is good, the breeze is cool and the sun is shining. Focus on the sounds you hear. Now, walk towards the edge of the mountain and put your feet on the edge. Look down and notice how everything looks tiny. Now, notice your feelings, walk slowly towards the centre of the building and don't forget your feelings, which you experienced when you were on the edge and looking down.

Now, open your eyes and take a deep breath. Relax yourself. Now, close your eyes and imagine once again that you are standing on the top of the same mountain as before. This time, you have beautiful, white wings and you are completely confident about your ability to fly due to these wings. You know that you are safe now. Notice what it feels like to fly; feel the wind rushing beneath your wings as you soar and glide effortlessly above the valley. Now, feel the freedom, and let yourself fly to your favorite place on the planet. It can be your favorite lake, city, woods or whatever you like. Be there and let yourself spend a few moments enjoying and do whatever you like. Notice your emotional and physical feelings.

Open your eyes after a few minutes .Realize that without any physical effort and without even leaving your place so felt/experienced all that. Similarly if you spend time in imagining bad/worse future events then actually you are responding to those images physically and emotionally therefore you attract those negative vibrations and circumstances in your life! Chose positive and uplifting images during visualization to create the vibrational match and to attract what you want.

Now do a comparison between your emotional and physical reactions during the two parts of visualization. Notice the joy, freedom, happiness and lightness in the first phase of visualization.

Vision Board/ Book

A vision board or a creativity collage is typically a poster board on which you paste images of things, people, money and success that you desire. It represents what you would like to be, having and do once you have achieved your goals. You can write the feelings with each picture that you would experience when you will achieve your goals. You can also use a book to paste and write on, which can become your map for the future; a tangible representation of where you are going. When your desires are represented with pictures and images it actually strengthens their vibrational level. Emotions are stimulated by visuals and pictures, and your emotions are the vibrational energy that activates the law of attraction.

> *"To visualize is to see what is not there, what is not real -- a dream. To visualize is, in fact, to make visual lies. Visual lies, however, have a way of coming true."*
> ~Peter McWilliams

You can use a vision board or a book for the representation of dreams for all the areas of life. Keep your life purpose in mind and use the list that you created for your dreams. Avoid chaos while making a vision board/book. Use only those words and images that represent you and your desires fully. Avoid too much information because it can distract you.

Spend some time, daily, looking at your vision board / book and visualizing. The best times are at the beginning and the end of a day. Visualization is best before going to bed because images during the last forty-five minutes before sleep repeat themselves in your subconscious mind during the whole night. The thoughts with which you begin your day are helpful in creating your desired future. When your dreams manifest then look at those images which you placed on your vision board and pay gratitude for them.

Create your vision board/ book every year because we all are growing and expanding every day. This will help you to stay motivated and focused. These beautiful pictures and images are representation of your future.

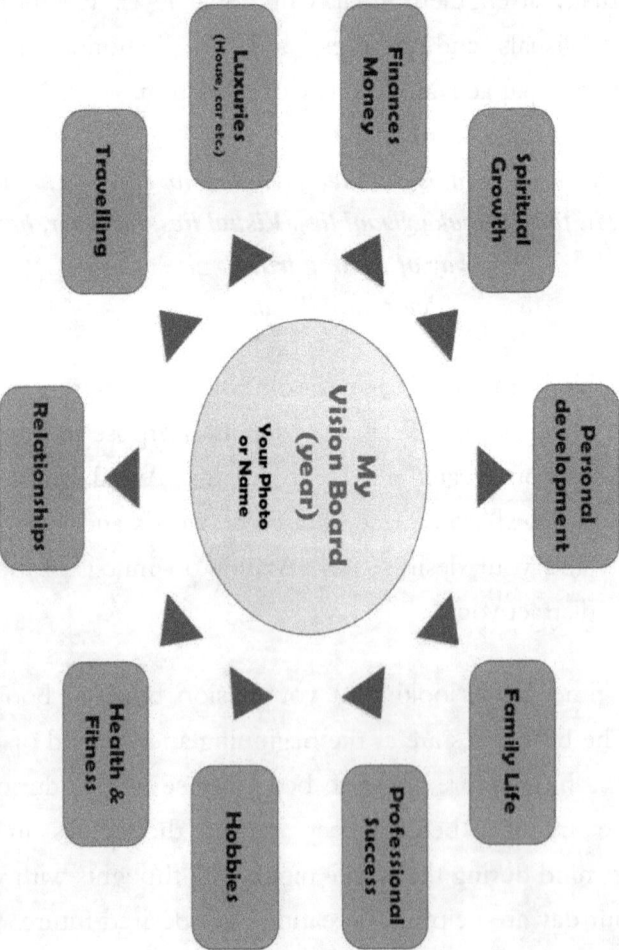

How to create your vision board

My Vision Board (year)
Your Photo or Name

- Luxuries (House, car etc.)
- Finances Money
- Travelling
- Spiritual Growth
- Relationships
- Personal development
- Health & Fitness
- Hobbies
- Professional Success
- Family Life

© Hina Hashmi

9. Taking Action

"Visualize, 'prayerize', 'actionize', and your wishes will come true."
~Charles L. Allen

Law of attraction doesn't teach that you shouldn't do anything to manifest your desires. Whatever you want to be doing or have you must make an effort for it. Dreams don't come true just by doing affirmations and visualization. Every desire/goal demands your best contribution mentally and physically. If you want money to buy a new car, you must look for opportunities for it however sometimes money can come from an unknown source. Sitting idle in your comfort zone, waiting for a miracle to happen cannot be the best way!

10. Allowing

"Think of this random Universe where everything is possible. The organizational skills belong to Law of Attraction. If you will relax and allow Law of Attraction to do the organization, the managing, then you can spend your time doing the things that please you."
~Abraham

To allow your desires to manifest, your vibration must be equal to the vibration of what you are asking for. All of your attention must be on what you really want.

When you ask for money, you shouldn't focus on the 'lack' by repeating the lack statements, such as "Money doesn't come to me easily." If you keep thinking about absence, you will not be able to attract it ever. Repetition of the lack story activates the vibration of lack, and then you don't get the money in the end. Only thing you will get will be negative emotions as an indicator of what you repeated. In this way you don't allow what you have asked for.

This is the most essential and easy-to-understand step in the attraction process. Imagine a situation: You ordered some food, and the delivery boy comes to deliver it at your place. You don't open the door to receive the delivery. Can you get that food without opening the door? The answer is NO. You must allow it in by opening the door. Similarly if we don't allow things we attracted; we don't get them.

The Art of Allowing is to deal with the gap between whom you are in the physical body and who you really are as an externally expanded spiritual being. All human beings are expanded versions of the source energy. When human beings generate ideas from preferences, desires, prayers or requests, non-physical energy follows those ideas and becomes equivalent to the vibration of that idea. Law of attraction just knows vibrations; everything that will match your vibrations will be attracted. That stream of energy moves forward towards the expanded version of me, the source that creates. Just release all doubts and resistances and focus on the positive aspects, then the stream will carry you towards the expression that you really are.

Ask and it is given –

> *"Ask, and it shall be given you; seek, and ye shall find; knock, and it shall be opened unto you: For every one that asketh receiveth; and he that seeketh findeth; and to him that knocketh it shall be opened."*
> ~*Matthew 7:7*

When you are focused on finding the best place for yourself, you will gradually achieve better and then the best. Your physical body becomes equal in vibration to the source within you. Now, you can see this world with the eyes of the higher self and feel it. That's the real experience of life.

When you were born, you didn't know how to select what should be stored in your subconscious mind. At that time, the ability to select wasn't developed.

The influential people program the minds of the children (e.g. parents, teachers, sibling, relatives ,etc.). The conditioning depends upon the belief system of those people. As a result of that 95% people are conditioned with limiting beliefs.

You were conditioned to accept many limitations which now stop you from attracting and allowing what you ask for. As mentioned earlier you should learn to change these beliefs and release fears which were created by other people in your life. Change your paradigm and be more positive to pull good things in your life.

"There is a Life Stream that flows to you, and this is a Stream of clarity, a Stream of wellness, a Stream of abundance - and in any moment, you are allowing it or not. What someone else does with the Stream, or not, does not have anything to do with how much of it will be left for you."
~Esther Hicks

11. Receive

Your task is to feel good because feeling good is the point at which you are on the frequency of receiving the best things, people and circumstances.

"Everything comes to us that belong to us if we create the capacity to receive it."
~Rabindranath Tagore

Your Notes:

SECTION NO: 4

The voice of our original self is often muffled, overwhelmed, even strangled, by the voices of other people's expectations. The tongue of the original self is the language of heart.
~Julia Cameron

Relationships
How to Make Yours' Fulfilled?

Relationships make you discover new talents and finding blocks that you cannot find yourself. Sometimes you have a circle of people who are supportive, helpful, optimistic and sincere while sometimes you feel frustrated by wounded souls. Every experience in the relationships is for some purpose which helps you to learn lessons of life.

"You cannot expect to draw people into your life that are kind, confident, and generous if you're thinking and acting in cruel, weak, and selfish ways. You must be what it is that you're seeking—that is, you need to put forth what you want to attract."
~Dr. Wayne Dyer

When the vibration fields of the people are combined or issues are identified we become aware of our feeling habits. You get opportunity of dealing with the people who are egoistical and always trapped in **I am me** and **You are you** because they forget that they are vibration beings and connected to everyone around them. A relationship creates a field around you which includes strengths, weaknesses, talents, potential and histories of both individuals. It creates a **collective self**. You can include wisdom of relationships, characteristics and lessons as a part of your own life. This is a perfect way of knowing your own self. When you include more people in the loop, it becomes a family, nation, organization, humanity and nonphysical dimension where everyone joins in a unified state. Only people who are on your frequency will enter your life.

If someone shows up in your life it is because they are on the same frequency as you and you are a vibration match. It's not necessary that you are both identical but you share some purpose. When you are together vibration field emerges and you share frequencies. It's true that you are similar to the people that you like but the fact is. You are also like people who irritate you and you don't like them. Use relationships for your transformation by recognizing the shared issues in partnership. Sometimes these are positive while some are negative.

"Learn to let your intuition—gut instinct—tell you when the food, the relationship, the job isn't good for you and conversely, when what you're doing is just right."
~Oprah Winfrey

Relationships are always evolved and are dissolved for the mutual benefits. As the law of attraction says, **Like attracts like**. Actually it depends upon your soul, whether it needs connection or not. If your soul doesn't require that relationship, then positive affirmations can't help in creating that relationship. When our soul resonates with people they appear in our field. When the resonation ends, they leave our lives. Required life patterns are always by the soul.

Sometimes we feel great attraction towards a number of people and it happens because we need to clear our blockage mutually. We tend to focus on our positive sides while few people are attracted to our negative pole to which we are stuck. We think sometimes opposites attract. In abusive relationships abuser and abused both are dramatizing a pattern to clear their hearts.

The only greatest tip for you is to allow the new relationships in your life. Stay calm and peaceful and trust the universe, whether you are searching for a life partner, friends, clients or other positive people that mean you are starting a new phase of your life. Now focus on maintaining the positive (True Frequency) of your soul. Imagine a big lamp of light above you which is sending you frequency nonstop, so positive people in your frequency can find you quickly.

Negative People can be a Blessing

"Throughout your life people will make you mad, disrespect you and treat you bad. Let God deal with the things they do, because hate in your heart will consume you too."
~Will Smith

We materialize many relations in life which are actually fear based. When fears of subconscious mind rule our actions we add people who share this kind of influence. Actually it's an opportunity to transform you. When two egos strike, those turn in to painful interactions. It can result in blame, punishment and rejection. Bad characteristics which you are seeing in other people and you don't like are actually a realization that's it's time to let go of **your own ego**. People don't realize the requirement of present time behave according to the orders of subconscious mind. Soul brings all those people in your life that have the same training of subconscious mind as yours have. When these negative relationships are developed, the main purpose is to dramatize a pattern to make it consciously reopen the heart.

"Each relationship nurtures a strength or weakness within you."
~Mike Murdock

Explore Yourself :

1. Make a list of qualities of people you wish to start a new relationships with?
2. Write a detail of every characteristic and expectation from that relationship.
3. Now activate the frequency of your new level of vibration. Imagine a white light rotating around your head.

Few people come into your life to release a mental or emotional fixation in the experience of your soul. If you have many phobias like animals, height, water and you find a partner who enjoys playing with the animals, going on a cruise and flying a plane, that person came in to your life to give an experience to your soul.

Your Notes:

When a Relationship Changes or Ends

"When you love a person you trust that he cannot go to anybody. If he goes, there is no love and nothing can be done. Love brings this understanding."
~Osho

People usually see end of friendships, marriage or other relationships as an expression of dishonesty or selfishness. When the vibration of the new person shifts, relationships can't be fulfilled. Ultimately people with totally different vibration disappear from your life. When someone's purpose in your life is over, he/she leaves immediately.

If one couple was totally living according to the rules of society and spending a routine life but suddenly one of them dwells towards spiritualism, at this point they lose a ground of being together because now the vibration pattern is totally different. Everyone has to pay the price of evolution. Maybe people call them selfish or they don't fit in to the rules of society. Evolution is a constant process and it's evident through our relationship whether close or professional. People who move out of synchronization and are low in vibration feel bad while coming out of old comfortable patterns. They try to use their force by blaming, being angry, complaining and proving others wrong and even to manipulate and physically abuse them.

If the partner or friends are open and communicative, they can talk about changes, discuss their dreams and goals in life, whether they are shifting or not. When both are ready to grow, relationships evolve and they again get synchronization. In order to keep relationships fluid and peaceful, friends or spouses must be honest and open for adjustments; otherwise misalignment can bring a shift and separation. If your partner rejects you or you come out of a relationship you can feel loneliness. Actually that's not loneliness, its alone time which your soul requires for your strength and transformation. You just have to stay calm, let go and be at peace. Allow your true frequency to take over your life.

"If people refuse to look at you in a new light and they can only see you for what you were, only see for the mistakes you've made, if they don't realize that you are not your mistakes, then they have to go."
~Steve Maraboli

Trust in your soul, it always give you everything that you truly need, whether it's a relationship or solitude. Never feel like you are alone because you are always with yourself. When your soul gives you more space at that time you can feel connection with divinity which is necessary. Feel the relationship with everyone around you, whether it's nature, your body, your soul, food, imagination and anything else surrounding you. You can feel love for the people who will connect with you in the future and thankful for those who moved out of your life to give you the space you need.

Strengthening yourself in this new phase of space is the main action required. Feel the love and joy everywhere instead of being stuck in the memories of previous relationships. Improve relations with the ideal partner, Divinity/Source/Higher Self/God/. Your real relationship is with your true self which is a part of Divinity. When you find someone who on a true frequency with you the relationship field becomes an extended field of expanded love, personality differences, any opinion or appearance no longer matter. They are always ready to understand each other. They are ready to laugh and feel joy because it comes from the soul and the inner child, which are pure. Both individuals are compassionate and feel safe with each other.

"Some of the biggest challenges in relationships come from the fact that most people enter a relationship in order to get something: they're trying to find someone who's going to make them feel good. In reality, the only way a relationship will last is if you see your relationship as a place that you go to give, and not a place that you go to take."
~Anthony Robbins

Other People in your World

If you and your partner give attention to a special kind of character, media, book or film then it means your soul wants both of you to pay attention to it. Your money oriented friends are actually giving you a signal of a new way in which you can be successful. For example a Husband reading romantic novels shows you both want more romance in the relationship. Sometimes we try to heal our wounds by healing the same kind of pain in other people. It cannot silence your pain. You need to heal yourself by letting go of your negative feeling habits. We all share the same field of consciousness and energy. When you heal yourself it heals your partner and everyone else in the field. Your healing is important for the whole universe. Our bodies and souls communicate with others telepathically. When you meet someone your body and spirits instantly match with their vibration and spirit is much faster in this regard. You can feel the waves of trustworthy people. You feel more peace in their presence.

"Radiate energy of serenity and peace so that you have an uplifting effect on those you come into contact with. Your presence will make others feel calm and assured."
~Dr. Wayne Dyer

© Maddy Malhotra

Explore Yourself :

1. Write down sensations of your body when you are with someone who accepts and understand you.
2. Write when your partner criticizes or judges you, doesn't understand or blames you?
3. When you meet someone new, how does your body respond?
4. What might I be learning from this person?
5. Am I reading the energy accurately?
6. What are the sensory clues? My body temperature? Their smell?
7. Is it a beneficial relationship or is it time to leave the relationship?

Your body is the best instrument which can tell you everything about other people, if you trust and start practicing.

Your Notes:

Your Notes:

SECTION NO: 5

That is the simple secret of happiness. Whatever you are doing, don't let past move your mind; don't let future disturb you. Because the past is no more, and the future is not yet. To live in the memories, to live in the imagination, is to live in the non-existential. And when you are living in the non-existential, you are missing that which is existential. Naturally you will be miserable, because you will miss your whole life.

~ Osho

Forgiveness
How to Make Peace with Your Past

"Forgiveness is one of the important keys to a happy and peaceful life. When people don't forgive themselves and others, they create an obstacle for the universe to provide them proper guidance for their lives. Often they can't receive or send positive vibrations and emotions. They can't get what they desire. True forgiveness is when you can say, "Thank you for that experience."
~Oprah Winfrey

It's been said that when you are unwilling to forgive someone, it's like consuming poison and waiting for the other person to die. So we must forgive negative people, and release painful circumstances from our lives. If we remove the effect of the negative memories from our past, we create space for a bright future to be created. When we forgive someone in our heart, it will ease us out by draining the negative out of us. It's a way for moving upward from lower frequency emotions of pain & anger to the higher frequency emotions like love.

"Throughout life people will make you mad, disrespect you and treat you bad. Let God deal with the things they do, 'cause hate in your heart will consume you too."
~Will Smith

Forgiveness is defined as:" To give up resentment against; stop being angry with; pardon; give up all claim to punish; overlook; cancel a debt". Forgiveness is a learned skill. We just don't know how to do this automatically. We can lean to empathize with other people when they are in pain by learning the art of forgiveness.

"Forgiveness is like setting a prisoner free. Once you have forgiven someone, you will discover that the real prisoner who has been freed is yourself, not the person who has hurt you."

~Anon

You become free of bitterness, and free to enjoy your present and your future. Forgiveness is a positive response to an injustice. It is goodwill, a merciful restraint from pursuing resentment or revenge. Forgiveness is paradoxical because it is natural for us to be resentful and we usually think that others should pay a price for their wrongdoing. Yes, the person who wronged us should pay for their deeds. They owe us something. The problem is there is no price high enough to pay for injustice. So we decide to cancel their debt anyway. Let the universe handle their karma.

"Forgiveness is the fragrance that the violet sheds on the heel that has crushed it."

~Mark Twain

Steps to Forgiveness

1. Write down the name of a person you wish to forgive.

2. Acknowledge how hurt you are, and even the hatred you may feel towards this person for what they have done.

3. Think of times in your own life when your bad actions have hurt or disappointed others. We also owe a debt we couldn't pay. None of us is perfect. None of us is faultless. It is much easier to forgive others, when we bear in mind our own weaknesses and failures. We are all in need of forgiveness from time to time. Maybe we have never committed something as awful as betrayal, but as long as we have an "I'm better than you" attitude, we will have trouble forgiving others. It is important to be honest with ourselves, and to view ourselves with sober judgment.

4. Decide you will bear the burden of the other person's wrongdoing. For example if your fiancé's/spouse's love affair is causing you tremendous pain, that's the burden. Be brave and decide you will face that pain, rather than running away from the issue. As you do, the pain will begin to subside.

5. Take a piece of paper and write: I forgive _____ (fill in the person's name) for _____ (write it all down) and it made me feel _____. Write as much as you need to.

6. Make a decision to forgive. Say it out loud, "I make a decision right now to forgive _____." Take as long as you need to, and be real. Ask for divine help if you need to.

7. Destroy the list: burn or throw it in a river. Get rid of it however you want.

8. Do not expect that your decision to forgive will result in major changes in the other person.

 9. Try to understand the person you have forgiven. What is their point of view? How do they feel? Why did they do what they did? What life experiences have they had that made them vulnerable to such temptation and wrongdoing?

10. Expect positive results of forgiveness in you.

Emotional Freedom Technique

EFT is a powerful, drug-free, easy-to-learn and easy-to-use technique that can reduce stress or painful emotions associated with thoughts, past experiences, etc. It was founded by Gary Craig. According to Traditional Chinese Medicine, there are several points on your body that can be tapped gently with the tips of the fingers on one hand, whilst repeating certain relevant phrases at the same time. This technique involves working with the body's energy field, or "meridians", so named by the ancient Chinese. Whether you believe in energy fields or not, you might be curious enough to try this the next time you feel negative emotions - and you'll be surprised by the results. This is the best technique for forgiving and letting go of negative experiences, people and circumstances.

To study it in detail visit www.emofree.com

Living in the Present Moment
Let Go of the Past

Everything that happened in the past served you to become what you are now. No one can predict the future events. What's gone is gone; that was your past. If you stroll around your past, the chances of getting the same kind of future are high.

Forgiveness means **letting go** completely without any strings attached. Things from the past that stay in your mind create aches in your head due to abnormal vibrations. You cannot acquire mental/emotional wealth if you are always thinking of the past like you cannot drive a car forward while looking in the rear view mirror. This is the most common habit among us.

Stop looking back on your life and wishing it was different. For pursuing that kind of mental activity will never lead to any worthy accomplishment. Think about what 'can be' rather than what 'was'.

Your Notes:

Resentment And Guilt
Life is either a Series of Endings or a Series of Beginnings

"Our fatigue is often caused not by work, but by worry, frustration and resentment."
~Dale Carnegie

Resentment is dwelling on something negative from one of the experiences from the past. Once can justify holding on to resentment but it's unhealthy. It is just deceiving yourself. A wise person will never do it. It is a mental act of ignorance. Holding it in your mind will make ones' vibrations negative. Resentment represents mental resistance to what has happened. It is like re-experiencing unhealthy past events again and again.

"Guilt is anger directed at ourselves - at what we did or did not do. Resentment is anger directed at others - at what they did or did not do."
~Peter McWilliams

Looking back on something you did which you thought was wrong and feeling bad about it in the present is known as **Guilt**. Resentment and guilt go hand in hand. Both the emotions affect your physical, emotional and spiritual health. Since you cannot change the past, guilt is inappropriate.

Affirmations to Release Resentment and Guilt
- I willingly release the thoughts and things that have clustered in my mind.
- I release the negative memories of the people for my highest good.

If you aren't successful in releasing then this means you aren't ready to release. If negative events happened in any area of your life then reframe those events in a positive way and write it. Keep your mind on high vibration images.

Gratitude
Thank for What You Have and Be Fulfilled

"Gratitude is the inward feeling of kindness received.
Thankfulness is the natural impulse to express that feeling.
Thanksgiving is the following of that impulse."
~Henry Dyke

Gratitude means giving thanks from your 'heart'. When you do this, energy flows from your heart and activates positive responses from other people as well as the universe. If you pay lip-service to gratitude or feel you ought to be thankful then your words and thoughts won't draw the same response.

When you feel thankful you are on the track of happiness and success. If someone has done nasty things to you then quite likely you would criticize and judge that person, you would feel angry, your body may feel tense or your head may ache. That is hell. There is a way out of hell to heaven. Recognize with compassion that people hurt you. Happy people do not do nasty things. Look for one good thing about them or one nice thing they have done to you. Focus on appreciating or being grateful for it. Their attitude towards you may or may not change but you will feel good again and that is heaven.

"For each new morning with its light,
For rest and shelter of the night,
For health and food, for love and friends,
For everything Thy goodness sends."
~Ralph Waldo Emerson

Manifestation process is fast and easier when a person pays gratitude for the things which he/she has in his dream list, imagining he has already received it or is in the process of receiving it. At that moment, he/she emits a powerful vibration. Each morning before getting out of bed pay gratitude for the great day ahead.

"Whatever you don't like and accept about the 'perfection' of your life right now will keep coming. What you believe is 'missing' will stay 'missing. Be grateful for however it looks and more will come to gratify you."
~Melanie Tonia Evans

I had a client who had many problems related to her mother. She couldn't forgive her for her bad behavior during her childhood and due to many suppressed emotions, my client had physical problems. I asked her to recall some positive things about her mother. Initially it was very difficult for her and she was reluctant. I suggested that she should make a list of the good moments she had with her mother since childhood and write a letter thanking her for those moments. She took one week for that task and then posted that letter to her mother. She was happy because gratitude and love took control of her life. Her relations with her mother were not good enough previously but after that letter full of gratitude, there was a prominent change in their lives.

Research shows that *"Most children's problems are related to their parents which can cause many physiological and psychological issues"*.

Gratitude can serve as a slow but effective treatment and gradually it becomes a part of life.

Thoughts and feelings of gratitude always emit positive frequencies. If someone just identifies and acknowledges the blessings in their life, a series of positive thoughts & frequency will be generated. Life of your dreams can become a reality just by paying gratitude for what you have. Ultimately you will get the results of your own desires. You just have to take the first step and then the law of attraction will draw more and more.

> *"Be grateful for what you have now. As you begin to think about all the things in your life you are grateful for, you will be amazed at the never ending thoughts that come back to you of more things to be grateful for. You have to make a start, and then the law of attraction will receive those grateful thoughts and give you more just like them."*
> ~Rhonda Byrne

There are so many victims of life around us, and they design their life in that way by focusing on the negatives and on what they don't have right now. Pay gratitude for even the tough and hard situations if you want to rise in your life. Actually these difficulties are stepping stone towards spiritual and emotional growth.

Always keep and carry something touchable in your purse or pocket that reminds you to pay gratitude. Hold it in your hands, close your eyes and be thankful for something, every time you hold it. By using this technique you can program your mind to think positive and enhance the frequency of your vibrations.

Due to absence and shortage of money people don't feel good about it. At this point there is one thing which can attract more money in life and that is gratitude. Stop for a while and be thankful for what you have.

"No matter where you are in life right now, no matter who you are, no matter how old you are it is never too late to be who you are meant to be."
~Esther & Jerry Hicks

Gratitude Journal

The best way of programming your mind to focus on the positive is to keep a notebook which can serve as your **"gratitude journal"**. Before ending your day write down all the good things that happened in that day. Moreover mention all the events in which the law of attraction worked for you.

You may write 5 small things like nice food you had or any other small things you are thankful for. Your continuous expression of joy will draw even greater joy, love and abundance into your life. Your focus will be programmed gradually. The Mind will start looking for positive aspects of everything.

The change in perception serves as a source of higher vibrations. Definitely the law of attraction will respond to these higher vibrations.

"Thank you' is the best prayer that anyone could say. I say that one a lot. Thank you expresses extreme gratitude, humility, and understanding."
~Alice Walker

Meditation
Preview of Life's Coming Attractions

*"I mean the whole thing about meditation and yoga is about
connecting to the higher part of you, and then seeing that every living
thing is connected in some way."*
~Gillian Anderson

The universe is communicating with us every moment. It guides us
for what to do and what not to do. It is essential to spend some time
away daily, be quiet and still, and listen to the voice of the universe.
It's a two way communication - whenever we pray the universe
replies but we rarely stop and focus on the answers. We just do one
way communication, by beating our own drum. It's like someone
puts the receiver down when you don't listen to the replies. Your
mind is full with your words, thoughts and beliefs but you are
constantly praying. Obviously you will get no response because your
mind will not let you listen to anything else.

*"Meditation has only one meaning, and that is going beyond the mind
and becoming a witness. In your witnessing is the miracle -- the whole
mystery of life."*
~Osho

The aim of meditation is to stop gossips and babbles going on in our
mind in order to allow the guidance and wisdom flow in to our
minds. We don't know the exact timings of divine response,
sometimes it's instant and sometimes it's not. We feel calm and silent
when the wisdom is being planted and it then takes some time to
grow out. We can find our true selves during meditation. Hell or
heaven is created by our inner world and with meditation we can free
ourselves from hell. The main aim is to silence your mind and it

263

doesn't matter whether you are sitting, lying, painting or walking in the nature. It can be anything which stops your mind from the routine chatter, so the divine message can be received. One simple technique for meditating is to focus on your breath, its movement in and out of the nostrils. Count from 1 to 6 while inhaling and 1 to 6 while exhaling. When your mind is still, repeat a mantra or the divine's names or chants.

Some examples:

1. **Om** (Hindu Mantra)

2. **Om manipadme hum** (Buddhist)

3. **Jesus Christ** (Christian)

4. **YaRehmanYa Raheem Ya Kareem** (Islam)

5. **Wah-E-Guru** (Sikhism)

Prayer
Learn to Talk to God and Unlock Your Spiritual Strength

"Prayer is more than meditation. In meditation, the source of strength is one's self. When one prays, he goes to a source of strength greater than his own."
~Madame de Stae

Prayer is a **communication** with God. God listens to us all the time, whether we realize it or not. Every single thought we have and every word we speak is actually a prayer. **Worry** is also a sort of prayer but you send a message of fear to God. Unknowingly, we use our energy/power to attract all that which we don't want. We must always focus our thoughts in the positive direction. Your style of praying is very important.

"Every prayer - every thought, every statement, every feeling - is creative."
~Neale Donald Walsch

The Elements of Prayer

1. The first element is the **communication** between God and us. This communication isn't based upon time and space because we are linked to the source. We don't need a satellite to send our prayers to the divine like a television requires. We don't need to wait for the results for days. It's instant but most of the time we are unable to understand the answer(s) because we aren't focused on listening to the replies. This communication is like a wire that connects two phone sets at two different places.

2. The second element is **energy**, which serves as the electric current flowing through the wire. This can be achieved by being mindful, concentrated and being in love. If you aren't in the present moment, you cannot pray irrespective of the faith. For the effective prayer, you must be present in the now because concentration is created by mindfulness, and without that, prayer is like a superstition.

How to Pray

"Prayer is not asking. It is a longing of the soul. It is daily admission of one's weakness. It is better in prayer to have a heart without words than words without a heart."
~Mahatma Gandhi

Faith is a prerequisite for an effective prayer. Ask with belief knowing that you will get whatever is in your highest good. People don't expect that their prayers will be answered so they don't even take action to achieve what they want. They are unaware that faith triggers response from the universe. God wants us to be happy but sometimes we don't get what we desire because we aren't ready to receive what we have asked for. We aren't ready to let go and wait.

This impatience stops our wishes from coming true. Be like a child who when demands toys from his parents trusts his parents and waits without panicking or feeling restless, disappointed, depressed or irritated.

Pray for some time, a week for example, and then stop asking. After some time, your prayers may automatically change because God has a different plan for your highest good unless you've got what you wanted.

Negative prayers for others always come back to you because sending negative energy will harm you the most.

Ask in your prayer and be detached from the result for some time. Pay gratitude to God for his response, have strong faith that something good will happen and be ready to receive.

Imagine if you are an HR manager and you want the highest good for every employee or potential employee who approaches you. Let us consider five scenarios: the first employee pleads like a beggar, moans and abases himself for an increment. You understand that he will soon waste his money and will ask for more money as loan. Second employee offers you some service or good in return for his promotion. You understand that he is making you a fool. Third, angry, employee threatens you that if he does not get a salary raise, he will kill himself. You know he is trying to manipulate you. Would you like to help them? The fourth, a depressed candidate for an interview, has limiting beliefs about his ability and lacks confidence but he wants a job for sure. You know if you will appoint him, he will never be able to do his work. Fifth person has some nice ideas and confidence in his eyes. He tells you how he can benefit your company. You will definitely select that person for the job. You support that person and his plans.

> *"Prayer does not change God, but it changes him who prays."*
> *~Soren Kierkegaard*

The most effective prayer is always from the heart, has purity of intention and believes that whatever happens will be in your highest good. God is so helpful and merciful. That's why He doesn't give us everything we ask for in our prayers. He knows that what we are asking for isn't in our favor. If you believe that God will always support you, you will notice that you are being helped in unexpected ways.

"Faith is knowledge within the heart, beyond the reach of proof."
~Khalil Gibran

Happiness
Realizing Your Potential for Lasting Fulfillment

Human beings have complete freedom to choose happiness. They have a complete potential to be happy or unhappy. These days happiness is unbelievable, if you say I am happy people will not consider you normal. It happens because we know the two options which trees and birds don't know the option of being unhappy. That's why they stay happy all the time. Usually people aren't happy because they lack harmony in the lives and they aren't joyful in whatever they are doing. Loving your work and way of living is also a sort of meditation.

Human beings always choose their ways but they aren't happy because they don't follow what they really love to follow. We are far away from nature and very much occupied with money prestige and power. There are very small things which can make you happy like song by a bird, a beautiful butterfly or cool breeze. These things can't give you power, money and prestige but can be a source of happiness. If you are real human being, choose your way and don't complain about that. Spending time with butterflies and flowers is your choice and you are not rich then are satisfied and happy about that. You can think that I am rich because I am happy.

People lose their inner self whenever they madly run after money, prestige and respect. They forget intrinsic values of life, happiness, joy and delight. Whenever they choose something from outside, they do a bargaining with themselves and when they gain without they lose within. Did they ever thought about a moment when they have conquered whole world and it's on their feet, they lost their inner treasure? What would they do with that money or wealth? People don't face their inner self and even don't know about it. May be a girl who is sitting in the office and dealing with the finance enjoys painting. How she can be happy? You must know your inner motives about life and keep on an eye on that and you will never be unhappy.

When people try meditations, recitations of religious mantras and prayers they have a relief from the pains but they help you to remain wherever you are, don't expect any major transformations in your life. Anybody can come out of misery but only condition is determination, while people do the opposite and talk about the misery all the time. They are happy to pay for that like visiting psychotherapist or counselor. When you realize that there is a misery in certain type of your life pattern that doesn't prove you wrong, actually that pattern is wrong. Your beliefs and patterns which you learned weren't actually good and helpful for you. Make your own decisions because moralities and orders of other people will cripple you.

Life knocks at your door to tell you what you should be or do. For example it wants you to be a poet but weren't ready to receive the message and wasn't present to listen (not open to receive intuition). You are hiding yourself behind someone else's mask, lost in grab of somebody else. Life search for you and it knows your identity and address but you always allowed the world to distract and disturb you. You can be lucky if you find your own element and real self, otherwise you cannot be happy. Happiness depends upon your choices in life. Few people consider pleasure as happiness which is actually a sensation. People struggle to achieve everything through body which is actually not possible. Each pleasure is balanced by the same amount of pain, while people are unaware about this fact. People aren't ready to face pain while running after momentary pleasures. Actually body exists in the world of duality i.e. day and night, life and death etc.

When people are in pleasure they are in fear of losing it, and when they are in pain actually they are in suffering and they put every possible effort to come out of that. This vicious cycle continues. People are running from one pleasure to another, actually running from one sensation to another. They are spending life without any depth. Happiness comes from quality not quantity it's psychological not physiological and it's not a relief from some kind of suffering because it's a sort of enrichment. This state can be attained by music during meditation or something beautiful in the nature. This is something much deeper and higher than the pleasure you gain from sex, food, money and relationships. The seeker of pleasure will remain at the mercy of winds and accidents without any independent existence because pleasure is always related to something else e.g. people, things, circumstances etc. When pleasure is associated with man, you are slave of him and you are in prison by your own choice.

Money and pleasure also a pleasure of few people, the more they get they become dependent on that because they have a fear to lose it and become reasonable due to this race. When the food is pleasure for you, soon you will get bored by the specific tastes because when it passes through the tongue you interpret it as pleasure. Gradually your taste buds will not respond to the taste and you will feel fed up. You can have the same experience when you are running after a man or women. One day you will make plans to get rid of that person because pleasure was exploring the new person once you know everything about him/her. You had a desire to have a huge bungalow, now you have it. Your mind will start seeking something else because there is no limit to pleasure seeking. People become victim of unlimited desires and become restless and neurotic.

A person seeking pleasure cannot be a sincere lover because he will definitely use other people as a mean for something and this is the peak of immorality. He has no other way instead of using humans and relations as tools. Cunningness is the requirement for the pleasure seekers otherwise they would be deceived because other people like them are ready to snatch. Happiness is more human and cultured than pleasure because that's not linked with physiological sensations because it's psychological in nature. Pleasure will come and go while happiness is timeless. Happiness isn't a good which you can buy or pursuit. People pursuing happiness cannot get it because it happens suddenly out of nowhere. Today when I was writing this chapter, I have seen a beautiful magpie outside my window and I was lost in its activities and that moment was full of happiness for me. Happiness is always available to you but when you see it you miss it. Desire of happiness moves you away from here and now because you move somewhere in the future which is a dream for you. It shows you aren't happy at the moment and a miserable being. The miserable person projects that someday he will be happy and forget that tomorrow is also his own projection of present self.

1. Don't dream about happiness and don't project because all happiness is today in this moment. You have the option to think about yesterday and become unhappier and same is the case with tomorrow. You have a gift of misery from the past because you loved someone very much and he insulted you yesterday and you are carrying that pain with you. You have the choice for being unhappy for the years. May be you have many questions like why did he insult me? Why did it happen to me? Even you were very loving and helpful. Yesterday no more exists and you are playing with something which no longer exists. Worry about finances in the future will lead you to the misery. What will you eat? Where would you live? You invite unhappiness. Living in here and now can stop unhappiness in your life because it's a natural phenomenon and surrounds you every time.

Universe is made up of happiness and joy like stars; sky and air are part of universe. You just have to look straightway instead of sideways, otherwise you will miss happiness. Happiness cannot be seen because it's your nature. Observe animals they are happy without status and money, trees are happy and blooming without any conditions; and their prayers, worship never stops. Only human being is unhappy creature because he is ambitious and doesn't live in the reality. Just observe a mother who loves her child but child wants more love and attention but mother's life has become horrible and disastrous. She tried to control her husband; moreover she is jealous and possessive. She isn't a loving woman how can she be loving mother.

People don't like happy person because it hurts their ego. They are surprised because they are unable to understand how that person came out of misery. Everyone is in the misery then how one person can be so strong and determined. Usually people don't dare to go against misery. Unhappy people are part of crowd but if somebody is happy he is individual.

The great happiness in this world is "being you". Human child is most helpless child in the whole animal kingdom because he cannot survive without the support of parents and other relations. Naturally, powerful people will mould him according to their own mind-set. Most of the people have the personality which is against their desires and they are pretending what they aren't. They were never allowed to be themselves and were forced to live according to someone else's rules and nature. They know that they have forced to become doctor, engineer scientist etc. Few beggars use children as commodities as the source of income, more or less everyone has been used as a commodity because it's happening with everyone at different scales. Nobody is happy because we are taught everything that tells him or her to not be themselves. They follow the rules which society, parents and peer teach them. This is the main cause of misery. They have to do something which they don't want to be, they have to marry someone whom they don't like. Society has programmed everyone to be miserable and it doesn't want anyone to show the misery. Eventually you have to come out of this misery and say, "I only want to be myself" and I cannot pretend to be someone else. This is a declaration of your freedom, stands you out of the crowd. Now you do not need any mask and be simply you. That's the beginning of real happiness

Joy:

Joy is spiritual and inner phenomenon and it has nothing to do with the outside. Basically it's a state of peace and silence.

Bliss:

Bliss is neither physiological, nor psychological nor spiritual. It's your innermost being where no ego exists. You can reach here just by dissolving your ego and following your truth. You cannot create or invent because it's the inner most part of yourself and it has been taken granted. The bliss makes you master and independent. To be really happy you need to be more conscious about yourself. Conscious person cannot be angry, possessive, greedy and ambitious. Consciousness releases energy involved in all above activities which was previously being wasted and you become a magnetic field which attracts all positive things in life. When you are conscious, meet the beyond of expectations that is the point of bliss, true happiness.

Children are being programmed for the competition from the early age. They are completely poisoned when they come out of university.

They learn that life is the survival for the fittest instead of considering it a celebration. The education system doesn't teach cooperation because it just teaches students to fight and be at the top. There is no training for loving, blissful and creative. Actually there is no guarantee of happiness even you are at the top. You have gone through a sort of misery while reaching at that place. Anxiety and tension are part of your life style because you don't know any other way.

The genuine education teaches you to enjoy whatever you are doing not for the results just for the act itself. If you want to do something genuinely like painting, dancing, engineering whatever you want to be. Drop your ego completely. The existence flows through your work and that's not a race because it's just a creation through you. An artist painting for fame has to defeat all other painters who also want to do the same. This approach brings your work at the secondary position because it's not your priority interest. Ultimately his work will be ordinary because he cannot do anything extra ordinary through competition.

Being happy on the expanse of someone else's happiness is inhumanity. Finding faults in others doesn't prove them wrong and make you right. Help others to be happy that will actually increase your happiness.

Your Notes:

SECTION NO: 6

You have everything you need for complete peace and total happiness right now.

~ Wayne W. Dyer

1. Acknowledgement

"Having a strong desire with strong doubt means your desire will not be manifested. Having a strong desire with just a little bit of doubt means your desire will come, though slowly. Having a strong desire with no doubt means your desire will be manifested quickly."
~Michael Losier

Doubt is the real cause of failure in the deliberate creation of your desires. Your task is to find out a way for removing it. How will you do it? You need to find out the examples of the people, circumstances, things and events to follow. The easiest way is to acknowledge when you find that the law of attraction has worked in your favor.

People don't feel happy when they manifest small things. They think that's not enough. When you attract any helpful information about 'how' you can achieve what you want then you should celebrate it. When you celebrate it, you offer vibrations which are closer to the vibration of your own target. Law of attraction doesn't have the power to analyze but it responds every time you worry, create, play, are happy, pretend or complain.

"Instead of focusing on the world's problems, give your attention and energy to trust, love, abundance, education and peace."
~Rhonda Byrne

2. Record Your Proofs

Keep a journal/notebook as a proof of the working of the law of attraction. Write down every manifestation, regardless of its size. You can raise your vibration by focusing on your achievements. The moment you find a proof of manifestation, doubt runs away. A loud voice within you will shout **"I believe"** and you will be able to listen to it. Getting rid of the devil named "doubt" will allow your desires to become reality. Then you will use the law of attraction more consciously. These confirmations will help you to trust the process more easily. Whenever you need to increase your faith in the law of attraction, read your journal.

"Know what you want, give it energy and focus, and become a scorekeeper. As a matter of fact, I encourage all of you that are going to follow this process with anything that you want to attract, is that you start keeping score - in the very moment. Say, "Hey, am I ever getting good! I attracted this. This is here because of me!."
~Michael Losier

3. I am in the Process of

Present circumstances are the actual competitors of your dreams. Whenever you focus on them you get distracted. When you focus on what you don't want, you offer a negative vibration. Cope with your negative thoughts and then replace them. Whenever you have a thought that you cannot manifest, tell yourself that you are always in the process of creating something. Are you not in a process? You are always in the process of creating something. You are experiencing events and circumstances as a result of the vibration you offer. Desires are never ending. The moment you think about something, you start a new process. So always tell yourself that you are always in the process.

I haven't attracted my ideal slender body; I am in the process of attracting my slender body.

"No one can deny you or grant you anything. It all comes to you by virtue of your vibration."
~Esther Hicks

4. Tell Yourself "A Lot can happen"

When we don't get what we want in the expected time duration, we think that maybe we need to wait forever.

People usually offer negative vibrations due to these kinds of thoughts.

Whenever you have same negative kind of thoughts, ask yourself:

1.Can something positive happen in the next few days?
2.Can A Lot happen in the next week?
3.Can A Lot happen in the next 30days?

The answer will always be "yes". Promise yourself that the moment you conclude a lack of results, You will focus on one thing "Lots can happen".

5. Ask for Helpful Information

Sometimes we make goals but we don't have enough information to achieve them hence we experience doubts while pursuing those targets.

Ask for the helpful information because It moves us towards our target. Helpful information keeps us motivated and optimistic about achieving our goals.

You can write:

I would like to start attracting information about how to get a new job.

I would like the law of attraction to bring to me some helpful information on how I can get the ideal slender body.

We have the least amount of resistance to information about our own desires. It comes easily, because we don't offer any negative vibration for it.

6. Attraction Box

It's a strategy to keep you hopeful. Make a box in which you can put your wishes. It can be a wooden, plastic or a cardboard box. When you see catalogues, brochures or flyers that have something you desire but you think you cannot afford it now then put them in your attraction box with the belief that your dreams, which are in your highest good, are going to come true..Now you are allowing all those luxuries & offers in your life. Take action and let the universes do the rest of the work.

7. Stay Away from How, Where & What?

We all put our energy into realizing our desires. There are few stages in life in which we don't have clear understanding of what to do. Most of us don't know how the universe works.

When you face any ambiguous situation, Stop here and say to yourself, "It's not my job; I am allowing the Universe/God/Higher Self to figure this out for me. You will know the right time to take action. Let the universe figure it out and you will start to get the answers you desire.

"There is a divine purpose behind everything - and therefore a divine presence in everything."
~Neale Donald Walsch

8. Hold Your Positive Vibrations

Negative people are energy vampires who have the capacity to lower down your vibration instantly. They usually talk about what they don't want. Your task is to change that 'don't want' conversation into 'want' conversation. Remember this tip while talking to them; otherwise they will lower your vibration by blaming and complaining. You will start realizing whose energy you like and who's you don't. Your inner voice will become your guide and will identify whether the other person is your vibrational match or not.

Always acknowledge the sources of abundance:

- You get a treat for lunch
- Free advice or coaching
- Gifts

- Free coffee
- Win prizes
- Discount or Sales Offers

"The Law of Attraction states that all forms of matter and energy are attracted to that which is of a like vibration. The implications of this law are vast, and the law holds true for all known Universes. "That which is like unto itself is drawn." The thoughts we hold attract similar thoughts and become large masses of thought called thought forms. The general vibration that a person holds is representative of the balance of their thoughts. As we become aware or conscious of our thoughts, we can raise our vibration by setting forth thoughts that are more in harmony with our desires. When our thoughts are in harmony with our highest desires, we are filled with joy and ecstasy. When we learn to set forth our thoughts consciously, we are no longer victims of our own outdated programming. We increasingly attract thought of a higher vibration and raise the level of thought at which we habitually vibrate."

~Esther and Jerry Hicks

9. Financial Success Exercise

Do this when you need clarity of desire and for improving the flow of money.

Develop an imaginary bank account.

Use an old notebook as check book, register and blank pieces of paper as deposit slip.

Deposit money ($100) in your account.

Spend it the next day at different places in the form of one check or another form.

Don't forget to fill memo portion e.g. bought a new dress.

Gradually increase you money deposit every day.

By doing this exercise you may find new ideas. Your point of attraction will be shifted. The Universe responds to your vibrations not the current state. When you focus on what you write, it moves you out of the fear of over spending. Desire has been placed in a no resistant state. So you are actually allowing it to flow.

10. Attract Wealth

"You will attract everything that you require. If its money you need you will attract it. If its people you need you'll attract it. You've got to pay attention to what you're attracted to, because as you hold images of what you want, you're going to be attracted to things and they're going to be attracted to you. But it literally moves into physical reality with and through you. And it does that by law."
~Bob Proctor

People usually focus on the lack of money instead of abundance. This exercise is to improve your feelings for money. You can do it when you have a shortage of money in your life. This exercise will help you to offer a vibration that will help you receive more money. It's like deception but for your mind.

Put $100 (or pounds) in your wallet or any amount convenient for you.

Keep it with you all the time.

When you touch your wallet feel the presence of money.

Think of all the things you could buy with 100 dollars, and focus on how happy this makes you

Wherever you go, whatever you want to buy, you can buy for this amount.

The purpose of this exercise is that you must feel abundant, because feeling the lack creates resistance for abundance to flow into your life.

"One of the keys of becoming more abundant is to be a deliberate sender of the vibration of Abundance. You see, abundance is a feeling. And the key to understanding that is that the Law of Attraction responds to the feeling that you're sending."
~Michael Losier

11. Exercise for Letting Go

Draw 3 columns, in the first write the goals you want to accomplish. In the second write what you want to do today and in the third write a to-do list for the Universe.

Goals	Achieve Today	Universe will do

Now just select items from the first column which are urgent and only you can do them.

You will feel relieved because you are now less burdened; allow the universe to let things happen for you. You will notice that the other side will also be shortened noticeably because your tasks will be accomplished gradually. It's all about the mindset because vibrations for worry and doubt hinder the processes of manifestation. When we let go things and don't stop the process by our negative vibrations then things happen smoothly and quickly.

12. Plan Every Segment of Your Day Positively

We are all, unknowingly, creating our future experiences every moment. We can choose to direct our intentions/expectations at any time. When we change our intentions we enter in to a new segment of life. Through this process we can consciously consider what we are projecting. We can take control of our future at any time.

When you get out of bed in the morning you enter in to a new segment, when you leave for the office, that's another segment. Decide your reactions to the expected situations before you enter in the next segment of your day. Set your intentions about the coming moment. How do you want to feel it? It's always helpful. When you feel difficulty in thinking about something or some scenarios, stop the process for the next moment. Think about something positive. Then continue again.

13. Learn to Quiet Your Mind

"The soul always knows what to do to heal itself. The challenge is to silence the mind."
~Caroline Myss

Learn to silence your mind, every day, for some time. It is essential to accelerate manifestation process. Add this silence to your daily tasks. Then, gradually, it will become easy for you to control your thoughts. If you are a beginner you may need three to ten minutes daily.
You are connected to your inner self because of this silence and quiet moments in which you have no/least worries, fears & doubts. You can listen to your inner voice easily. This process will change you from within by changing the brain wave patterns which will ultimately create happiness, and good feelings will increase automatically. Humans are spiritual beings and their connection with eternity is in their very nature. That connection is facilitated through meditation. It's a tried and tested tool to seek unlimited wisdom.

According to some people through prayer we talk to the universe, while through meditation we listen to it. It frees us from worries, tensions and negative thoughts, and the place for joy, bliss, happiness and love happens.

"Our thoughts create our reality - where we put our focus is the direction we tend to go."
~Peter McWilliams

Maintaining Focus is a basic prerequisite for developing the intuition and materialization process. Nowadays a lot of people have short attention span due to the development of technology. That's not their fault completely, they are habitual and programmed for it. Focus can be maintained by practicing meditation.

Explore Yourself :

1. Give your inner-self a symbol, it can be anything: a star, a ray of light or any shape.
2. Visualize a small screen in front of you.
3. Imagine the symbol (from step 1) on the screen and focus on it; does it change color and/or shape?
4. Feel it in your mind and try again after a few minutes.

Your Notes:

14. Identify Your Feelings

We must monitor our thoughts regularly to keep track of our feelings. It must be done multiple times a day. Just stop yourself and ask, "How do I feel in this moment?" You can be more aware of your emotional states by doing this.

> *"Like food is to the body, self-talk is to the mind. Don't let any junk thoughts repeat in your head."*
> *~Maddy Malhotra*

If someone claims that he always thinks good thoughts but feels bad most of the time, he is most likely lying because feelings are created by thoughts. Our frequency (like radio frequency) is determined by our thoughts. Our feelings are indicators of positive and negative energies.

Feeling bad is an indication of negative thoughts. Your bad feelings act like a magnet and invite more bad feelings/things in multiple areas of your life.

Calm yourself down for a few minutes and come back to your neutral state. You can do it by simple meditation or by being thoughtless for a while. Your bad feelings are cautions from the universe to "Change your frequency by changing your thoughts right now". When your frequency is higher and more positive, pictures of your life will change. With positive thoughts the experiences of your life will change into greater ones.

15. Clear Pictures of Your Desires

Your desires must be identified properly by the help of **intuition** and then ask for them only once. Once you have asked then let it happen. Wait for the response from the universe. If you go to a restaurant and order a meal, would you call the waiter again and again to ask about the progress of cooking etc.? You don't have to ask over and over again, just ask once. It's just like placing an order from a catalogue. You don't place the same order again and again. You order once. Get clear about what you want and then ask for it with faith.

"Your vision will become clear only when you can look into your own heart. Who looks outside, dreams; who looks inside, awakes."
~Carl Jung

16. Internal and External Nudges / Guidance System

Excitement is the indicator that you are on the right track and in alignment with your real self. When you have to make decisions, listen to your intuition and follow your feelings instantly. For example, if you get a feeling that you must do something, do it. That's your intuition which is guiding you. The Universe gives us messages, it communicates with us all the time. It's totally up to us whether we accept the messages and act on it or not.

"The device for external nudges is the resistances which we encounter many times during different times in life. Nothing works, even when we try hard. It tells us that we are on the wrong track. We must change our point of attraction or change our desire. If we allow these nudges to guide us, they will. The Universe is responding to who you feel you are."
~Esther Hicks

17. Inspired Action

If you are making conscious efforts to materialize something, it will add anxiety to your life. That's a big obstacle for manifesting. The inspired action is to act like a receiver because you are on the frequency of receiving what you have asked for. It is effortless and you feel like you are on course by being positive and controlling your emotions, thoughts and vibration. If you keep your vibrations high, manifestation will happen as smoothly as a river flows.

18. Actions Must Be Mirroring What You Expect To Receive

If you are expecting to receive something your actions must be in concordance with the desire. You should behave in a way that can express the expectation which you have in your mind. If your dreams come true today, what will you do? Take actions which can reflect that powerful expectation.

19. Respect Yourself

There is one human being who deserves your love and respect the most and that's you. If you wish that other people must treat you with respect and love, then you have to respect yourself first. When you respect yourself, your frequency emits a signal that you deserve love and respect from other people. The behavior of people towards you is just a reflection of your repetitive thoughts.

"To free us from the expectations of others, to give us back to ourselves - there lies the great, singular power of self-respect."
~Joan Didion

20. Give Yourself

"Love yourself first and everything else falls into line. You really have to love yourself to get anything done in this world."
~Lucille Ball

The desire of worthiness can be fulfilled by putting yourself first. Most people habitually put themselves last. As a result of that they attract more feelings and situations creating worthlessness for them. You can give to other people when you yourself already have enough. Unless you fill yourself up first, you have nothing to give anybody else. Joy is a state of natural flow which is attained by giving yourself first.

21. Manage stress

"God will never give you anything you can't handle, so don't stress."
~Kelly Clarkson

An important key to manifestation is your control over your thoughts. When you leave even one negative thought unhindered, it attracts more negative thoughts, which results in the manifestation of stress. The main cause of stress is negative thinking. You can change it by choosing to think positive.

22. Think Yourself Young

You can choose to feel yourself young in your mind. This is connected to our beliefs. According to medical science, we have a brand new body every few years. You can feel good by telling yourself that your body is only a few years old. You must celebrate every birthday as your first birthday.

23.Emit a New Signal With Your Thoughts

"Remember that your thoughts are the primary cause of everything. So when you think a sustained thought it is immediately sent out into the universe. That thought magnetically attaches itself to the like frequency, and then within seconds sends the reading of that frequency back to you through your feelings. Put another way, your feelings are communication back to you from the universe, telling you what frequency you are currently on. Your feelings are your frequency feedback mechanism!"
~Jack Canfield

Forceful attempts to change your life won't change your life, positively, in the long run. If you want to change something, you will have to change your thoughts and feelings to change your frequency. That act will emit a new signal which will create a new picture of your life. If you oppose what you don't like, you are making them more powerful by adding more energy to it. You will attract the unwanted things more and at a faster rate.

24.Avoid Negative Energies

We have manifestation equipment in our head and that is our 'mind'. It has the ability of processing the pictures which enter in it. Avoid watching and reading negative news. We rush for them when we see hypnotic headlines. News keeps our focus on the negative hence we attract more negativity.

25. Create your Life Intentionally

Time passes so fast that's what most people complain about these days. If you calm down and tell yourself that you have plenty of time to manage everything you want, then everything will be possible in the same amount of time. Plan everything before time; let the universal forces work for you. Make it a daily routine.

Explore Yourself :

Sit in a comfortable position, close your eyes if you like, keep your body relaxed throughout. Think of a nice place, recall a happy memory or listen to a sound around you. If your mind wanders, gently bring it back to the point of concentration. Your focus will improve with practice. Next point is observation; you have to behave like a neutral observer without judging anything. Your observations can be memories, worries, planning, images etc. Imagine you are surrounded by bright white light which is protecting you. When you are surrounded by light, visualize your future. Visualize the kind of people, circumstances, events and targets you want to manifest. Repeat it in your mind as it is your current reality.

Your Notes:

26. Replay Your Day

One of your daily rituals must be to replay all the activities of that day. The benefit of this habit will be the removal of all negative events and the things which were not the way you wanted. Now visualize your time in the way you want it. This is a method to remove all negative & unwanted frequencies from your day. In this way new frequencies can be emitted easily. It's a very entertaining way to design your destiny. Hurry up and take control of your future life. If you had a fight with someone and you felt anger then replay that event in your mind and change into positive experience in visualization that will remove the negative stuck energy.

27. Giving

"Life is a gift, and it offers us the privilege, opportunity, and responsibility to give something back by becoming more."
~Anthony Robbins

Giving is a great way to attract what you want in your life. Most of the wealthiest people are great philanthropists. If you think you don't have enough money to give, start giving. As you demonstrate faith in giving, the law of attraction will give you more to give. If you want love, start loving people. Remember one thing though; give it from your heart not out of greed. It should not be given with an expectation of getting back.

28. Act as You Already Have

Think about what you have asked for and make sure that your actions mirror what you expect to receive, and they don't contradict with what you asked for. Do exactly what/how you would do if you were receiving it today, and take actions in your life to reflect the powerful expectation. Make room to receive your desires, and as you do, you send out a powerful signal of expectation.

29. Love Yourself

"You can search throughout the entire universe for someone who is more deserving of your love and affection than you are yourself, and that person is not to be found anywhere. You yourself, as much as anybody in the entire universe deserve your love and affection."
~Buddha

We must **'feel good'** to use the law of attraction in our favor. Feeling good can transform your life and the universe. You can bluff with yourself but not with vibrations. The universe designs according to some laws. An important tip for feeling good is to start loving yourself. When you feel good about yourself, you open yourself up to all the love and all the good that the universe has for you. Having a big ego and narcissism are unhealthy and do not come with any benefits ultimately.

Good things, including health, wealth and relationships have similar frequency as joy, happiness and feeling good. Feelings of having unlimited energy and of wellbeing are linked with happy feelings. When you love yourself, you will probably attract more loving people, circumstances and situations that will, in turn, become a source of life satisfaction and happiness.

299

When you focus on the positive aspects of yourself then the laws of attraction will continue to show you more good things about yourself. Sit comfortably for few moments at any point during the day, take a few deep breaths and just focus on something positive about yourself.

30. Focus on the Positive

"You must remain focused on your journey to greatness."
~Les Brown

Majority of people focus on what they don't want rather than focusing on the positive results they want. The mind works using images. These images get stronger depending on the strength of the emotions behind them. If happy feelings and images are in your mind, you will receive more happiness. Humans are the most powerful creatures who can emit a new signal anytime they want just by shifting their focus. The universe responds to that. By shifting your focus you emit new signals. These new signals of love, peace and happiness have all the powers to draw same emotions and experiences into your life

31. Praise and Bless Others

A powerful act for attaining the highest frequency (love) is to praise and bless everything in your life. In this way, you involve the divine in your life and move towards prosperity and wellbeing. So begin right now to invoke the power of blessings in your life, and bless everything and everyone. Likewise with praising, when you praise someone and/or give love, you emit that magnificent frequency and it will come back to you. Praising and blessing dissolves all negativity, so praise and bless your enemies. If you curse your enemies, the curse will come back to harm you.

"I praise loudly. I blame softly."
~Catherine the Great

To trust in the force that moves the universe is faith.

Faith isn't blind, it's visionary.

Faith is believing that universe is on our side, and that the Universe knows what it's doing.

~*Anon*

Congratulations!

You have taken the first step and now understand how life works. You are much better than those who don't try to find out the answers about life. They moan about their bad luck, feel helpless and spend their lives in self-pity and blaming others. Our circumstances don't change just by praying, weeping and staying depressed overnight. We need to make an effort and take action to improve our lives. Learn the lessons which the events in our live teach.

Now you have learnt to understand why something is happening to you and how paradigm shift and reframing of the thoughts about an event can keep you calm, peaceful and happy. When you learn to flow with the life you can easily attract what you want because you know how to get rid of mental blocks and enhance your personal vibrations.

When you need help to take the next steps to happiness, fulfillment, joy, wealth and wellness, then contact me and I will be your guide. I will be very happy to help you on your journey.

I wish you a Wealthier, Happier, Love-filled, Healthier and Peaceful life!

Hina Hashmi

Hina Hashmi
www.BeHappyandPeaceful.com

Suggested Reading

If you wish to understand/achieve:

- ✓ Self Beliefs
- ✓ Emotions
- ✓ Habits
- ✓ Fears
- ✓ Positive Attitude
- ✓ Self-Esteem
- ✓ Confidence
- ✓ Leadership Skills

Then I would recommend Maddy's best-selling book *"How to Build Self-Esteem and Be Confident: Overcome Fears, Break Habits, Be Successful and Happy"*

One to One Coaching

If you are committed to make your life better then I will help you to understand how life works, attract wealth, soul mate and ideal body, have Joyful relationships, inner-strength and self-Love, and support you to set goals and hold you accountable whilst fully believing in you, so <u>you can</u>

- ✓ **Attract what you want** instead of attracting what you don't want.
- ✓ **Feel good** by achieving your **ideal body shape**
- ✓ Have **fulfilling relationships** and have **more time** for your family and yourself
- ✓ Learn to listen to your intuition and seek inner guidance to enhance decisions making skills.
- ✓ Understand how to resolve the 3 biggest mental blocks: negative self-beliefs, self defeating thoughts and unhealthy emotions.
- ✓ **Increase** your **income** to **enjoy** the luxuries you wish
- ✓ Have a **positive attitude**. Make better decisions.
- ✓ Discover how to let go of negative energy by using powerful tools like forgiveness, gratitude, prayer and meditation
- ✓ Experience more **happiness, peace** and **fulfillment**
- ✓ **Progress** in your **career** or business

When you are ready to increase happiness and peace in life , then email me with some details of what you would like to achieve: hhashmi@live.com or read more details about my coaching services on: www.behappyandpeaceful.com

Migraine Cure

"Long term relief from migraine is possible."

If you are open and motivated to try something different (psychotherapy/alternative therapy) then I can help you to get rid of vicious cycle of pain, medicines or caffeine intake. So you can:

✓ Feel more **energetic**
✓ Have better problem solving skills
✓ Have more **peace** of mind.
✓ Be more **relaxed**. It means levels of stress will reduce and have positive impact on their physical and emotional health.
✓ Some people even have a **high self confidence**.
✓ Have better mood and **good tolerance** level because frequent spells of pain can make a person irritable and intolerant which affects relationships at home and work place.
✓ Pain free life brings a **paradigm shift** in some peoples' lives

When you are ready to get long term relief from migraine headache, then email me : hhashmi@live.com or read about my service on: www.migrainecure.co.uk

www.ingramcontent.com/pod-product-compliance
Lightning Source LLC
LaVergne TN
LVHW051038080426
835508LV00019B/1593